WHY
DOES
A NICE GUY
LIKE ME
KEEP GETTING
THROWN IN
JAIL?

How theological escapism and cultural retreatism in the church have led to America's demise.

by Randall A. Terry

Huntington House Publishers
&
Resistance Press

Huntington House Publishers
P.O. Box 53788
Lafayette, Louisiana 70505

&

Resistance Press
P.O. Box 600
Windsor, NY 13865

Library of Congress Card Catalog Number 93-78791
ISBN 1-56384-052-9

Dedication

To my children.
And to their descendents.

CONTENTS

We know ourselves to be one with our people in a great company of suffering and in a great solidarity of guilt. With great pain do we say: Through us endless suffering has been brought to many people and countries. . . . We accuse ourselves for not witnessing more courageously, for not praying more faithfully, for not believing more joyously, and for not loving more ardently.[1]

Leaders of the German Evangelical Church,
October 1945

Introduction

You will never be the same after you read this book. You may laugh, you may cry, you may be happy, you may be mad, but you will not be the same.

After nearly fifteen years in Christian ministry, I have been through more ups and downs, more battles (and certainly more jails!) than most Christians will go through in a lifetime. As I have observed the church throughout the second half of the seventies, the eighties, and now the nineties, I have been hopeful at her potential yet troubled, dismayed, and even broken-hearted at her inability—or unwillingness—to stand for God and His Word in our nation and to impact the culture at large.

Why? Why do the heathen rage around us, and our response is timidity, silence, retreat, or some worn-out pat answer—"It's going to get worse in the last days," or "We're just called to preach the gospel"?

I have looked for crippling first causes and flimsy first principles in the church's theology that have aided in America's demise and strengthened our enemies' hands. I have laid them out succinctly, with humor where I could, to provoke you into reexamining some current mass-marketed, mass-accepted theology—theology that at its best is error. At its worst, it may have been slipped into our ranks by hell itself.

I have also given quotes concerning the church in Germany during the 1930s which give an overview of the Nazis' clear goals, and the German churches' theological compromise and cultural cowardice that facilitated the Nazis' success. The parallels between the German churches' lack of resistance to the Nazis and the American churches' lack of resistance to the pagan elite of our day are truly frightening. The theological sand that much of the church in America is built on today seems to have passed from Nazi Germany through the hourglass of time safely into America's seminaries, churches, ministries, and homes.

Perhaps we can rid ourselves of some of this out-of-balance, debilitating theology. Perhaps my feeble attempt to point out the emperor's nakedness will strengthen you to do the same.

I'll bet a brawl is coming with the emperor's clothing manufacturers.

Enjoy the book, and pass it on.

Randall A. Terry

Do you really believe the masses will ever be Christian again? Nonsense! Never again. That tale is finished. No one will listen to it again. But we can hasten matters. The parsons will be made to dig their own graves. They will betray their God to us. They will betray anything for the sake of their miserable little jobs and incomes.[1]

Adolf Hitler (in the first months of his power)

The clergy believed that their hold over their people was safest from within the bastion of the Church's stronghold. They did not perhaps realize that they could also be imprisoned therein.[2]

One

IN THE SLAMMER

(I'm Back in the Saddle Again)

There I was again—in the slammer. I was stuck in
Wichita, Kansas, during the historic "Summer of Mercy."
My wife and children were about to go back to upstate
New York. Before they left, they were going to pay me
one last visit. They were supposed to arrive for a visit
about noon. They didn't arrive until after one o'clock.
They got lost.

When they finally arrived, Captain Smith took me out
of my cell, down the winding, barred hallway. He showed
me the normal visitation rooms. The prisoner sits in one
room, the visitors in another, and a thick, cold piece of
Plexiglass separates them. They communicate through a
little obnoxious metal screened hole that muffles and
distorts their voices. Thankfully, I was spared this heartache. I couldn't wait to hug my children and hold my
wife's hand. I rounded a bend, and there were Cindy and
the children in a concrete entryway. The captain took us
to a private office and left us alone for thirty precious
minutes. I thanked God for the captain's kindness.

"Visiting" my family as a prisoner varies between
pleasant, difficult, and gut-wrenching, depending on the
situation. On this occasion my wife laughed and my kids
giggled when they first saw me. They didn't think it was
funny that I was in jail—but they did think my uniform
was hysterical. My daring new outfit was comprised of a

flaming orange short sleeve pull-over top and flaming orange boxer shorts—complete with designer rubber sandals.

But this wasn't a joke, and the grins about my wardrobe quickly disappeared. Cindy's eyes showed signs of the tears she cried on the way. (It hurt me to think of her crying as she drove away.) My daughter Shawn just sat on my lap and clung to my neck. She was quickly joined by her sister Elizabeth (one little girl sat on one knee; the other little girl sat on the other). They were five and six years old, respectively. Alan, who was eleven years old, didn't say much. He just sat next to me trying to be brave, fighting back the tears. He remembered other jail experiences; he knew what might be ahead.

We laughed and talked and prayed for a whole thirty minutes together—which was twice the normal visitation time. The captain had mercy on us because he knew they were going back east, and I might not see them again for a long time.

Shawn proudly showed me her first loose tooth. I was sure it would be out before I was. Elizabeth happily displayed her first missing tooth, with two others promising to wobble out soon—her little fingers expediting the process.

We homeschool both of the "little girls," as we call them. While I was entrenched in the "Summer of Mercy," they were both just learning to sound out words phonetically. Cindy recounted to me her amazement at how quickly they were learning to read. I looked at them both and said, "You two aren't really learning to read that fast, are you?" my voice tempting them to prove me wrong.

I wrote out D . . . A . . . D and listened with joy as Shawn methodically sounded out a consonant, a vowel, a consonant, and then turned to me all smiles, exclaiming, "Dad!" Elizabeth quickly repeated the lesson when I wrote out M . . . O . . . M. "Mom!" I tickled them and laughed with them and told them how brilliant they were.

Then I put Shawn to the test: "Write out, 'I love you,

Dad.'" I watched in amazement as she sounded out, "i luv u dad." It broke my heart.

While I was clowning around with the little girls, our eleven-year-old son sat quietly for most of the visit. I tried to strike up conversation with him, but he didn't feel like talking. He was upset about my being in jail—again. When our half-hour was up (I thank God for every minute), I gave him a long hug and said, "Pray for me. Be brave, be strong. Be a good help to your mother." As he walked out ahead of me, Elizabeth kept asking, "Mom, why is Alan crying?"

Cindy whispered to me that Shawn cried herself to sleep the previous night because I was in jail. I was sure there would be a lot of crying before this was over.

I ached inside as I watched them leave. "Bye, Daddy! Bye, Daddy!" The voices of the little girls echoed in the dingy, cold, cinder-block lobby.

I waved half-frantically. "Good-bye, children! Good-bye, honey! God bless you! I'll miss you. I love you!"

The officer led me back to my isolated cell. The closing thud of a barred metal door has an incredibly permanent sound.

I wondered how long I would be in. Maybe five days. Maybe five weeks. Maybe five months. Maybe five . . . no, stop Randy. I couldn't bear the thought. It couldn't happen. My imagination was running away with me.

The Prisoners of the Lord

May God bless the Chinese Christians, Soviet Christians, and other dear saints in this generation who have endured jail and separation from their families for years. We cannot imagine the anguish of soul, the longing for loved ones, the incredible price they have paid for obeying God.

I have begun this book in this manner to paint for you the physical and emotional setting in which I started to write it. Perhaps you will understand a little better why I am so forthright in my challenge of certain out-of-balance theologies. Perhaps you'll extend me a little grace for my bluntness.

Moreover, I have made a feeble attempt to give you a glimpse of the heartache that can accompany incarceration—especially lengthy incarceration. Not so that you'll feel sorry for me, but so that you will "remember those who are in prison as if you were their fellow prisoners" (Heb. 13:3) and stand with them at home or abroad.

If a Christian in your area is jailed for righteousness' sake, don't forget him (or her). Pray for him, and do all you can to comfort and aid him and his family during his time of distress. If you learn of Christians in jail in another state or nation, petition officials by letter or phone on their behalf for their release. Jesus receives it as if you were caring directly for Him (Matt. 25:36-40). Conversely, if we neglect and forget our brethren in jail, Christ feels as if we have neglected and forgotten Him (Matt. 25:43-46).

And finally, if we don't get our act together, a lot more Christians are going to find themselves behind bars in America. If we don't wake up soon in freedom, we may wake up in jail.

The Führer, they said, was "the redeemer in the history of the Germans. Hitler stood there like a rock in a wide desert, like an island in an endless sea. In the darkest night of our Christian church history, Hitler became for our time that marvellous transparency, the window through which light fell on the history of Christianity."[1] And "We put our trust in our God-sent Führer who was almost blinded when he heard God's call: 'You must save Germany', and who, once his sight was restored, began that great work which led us to the wonderful day of 30 January 1933."[2]

The "German Christians"

Since yesterday our German people have been called on to fight for the land of their fathers in order that German blood may be reunified with German blood. The German Evangelical Church stands in true fellowship with the fate of the German people. The Church has added to the weapons of steel her own invincible weapons from the Word of God: the assurance of faith that our people and each individual is in God's hand, and the power of prayer which strengthens us in days of good and evil. So we unite in this hour with our people in intercession for our Führer and Reich, for all the armed forces, and for all who do their duty for the fatherland.[3]

German Evangelical Church, 2 September 1939

In the circumstances, therefore, it is not surprising that the most terrible outrage of the whole Nazi era—the attempted extermination of the Jews, with all its attendant horrors of mass murders and gas-chambers—was not loudly and urgently denounced by the Churches. . . . All save a handful of German churchmen continued to turn a blind eye on events.[4]

Two

VISIT FROM THE THEOLOGICAL TWILIGHT ZONE

(The Lights Are On, but Everybody's Out to Lunch)

It was eerie—like a visit from the twilight zone.

I was trying to get over missing my family, trying to settle in for what might have been a long haul.

And then they came.

I had just begun reading *The Nazi Persecution of the Churches, 1933-1945,* when two Christian brothers came by on their volunteer "chaplain visits." Judging from the lines etched in their faces, I would guess they were in their late sixties or early seventies.

Once they realized who I was, they quickly dispensed with preliminary niceties and were bold enough (dare I say calloused enough) to point out to me the reasons why those of us involved in Operation Rescue were wrong for our actions. Most of their protests could be used to speak against all "Christian activism." It was truly frightening to hear them talk, especially in the light of *The Nazi Persecution of the Churches.* In a matter of five minutes, they unwittingly outlined a host of foundational problems in the church. These are excerpts of the little fake pearls of wisdom they slipped me through the bars. (Anybody who has heard me speak or read my writings can guess my responses.) This is the gist of what they said:

"You can't expect those pro-chance people—what do you call them—pro-*chance*?" he asked. "No, pro-choice," I explained. (I knew then I was in for an earful. I actually became eager to hear.)

"Oh yeah, I get those words mixed up. Anyway, you can't expect those pro-choice people to change from protests."

"I don't believe God would have us use force to change their minds. He just wants us to pray."

The other man chimed in. "I just wish you could do things a little different. I mean, you read about it in the paper. . ." He paused while he thought of how he could say it. "I wish you could do things *in a way that doesn't give Christians a bad name . . .*"

"I think it's wrong if Christians get together and say we can shut down their business if we get enough people. My son and I have a business, and we wouldn't want Christians to try and shut it down. . . . I don't think it's right to try and close down a doctor's legal business. If you try to close down their business—well, they're going to call the police."

The other man started back in. "*I believe we need to share the gospel.* The Lord can change their hearts. You're probably really missing an opportunity down there to share the Lord with them."

"After many years in Christian ministry, I don't believe the Lord wants us to use force. . . . They aren't Christians you know—they don't believe it's a life."

The other said, with solemn confidence, "I think things are going to get even worse before the Lord returns."

We politely bantered back and forth, and once they had expended all their rhetorical ammo (with obviously no success), they slipped back into the prepared text and gave the crowning line: *"Have you ever received a Gideon's New Testament?"*

These "from the hip" one liners—as innocuous as they may seem—are a profound revelation of the state of Christianity in America during the 1990s. Their best shots reveal some of the worst spots in American Christendom.

Each of their flimsy statements has a hard (or should I say soft-headed) theological core which is extensively taught in most of our seminaries, marvelously expounded upon in most of our pulpits, and flawlessly lived out in most Christian lives. These are some of the reasons why a nice guy like me keeps getting thrown in jail. These are reasons why the Church is in great jeopardy. These are some key reasons why America is plummeting into chaos. These are the reasons why your liberties are in danger.

I am going to lead you through a blunt, brutally honest look at the theological sand upon which these flimsy statements were based. The cultural, familial, political, and ecclesiastical fruit of some of this nonsense is nothing short of calamitous. So forgive me if I don't pull too many punches. There is an awful lot at stake.

It is my purpose neither to re-erect in the forests of Germany heathen altars and introduce youth to any kind of Wotans-cult, nor in any other way to hand over young Germany to the magical arts of any herb-apostles. . . . I promise the German public that the youth of the German Reich, the youth of Adolf Hitler, will fulfil their duty in the spirit of Adolf Hitler, to whom alone their life belongs.[1]

Baldur von Schirach

Christianity and Nazism are like fire and water. We must not yet say this openly. Outwardly we must not attack Christianity, we must be far more clever; we are not interfering with denominational matters, but with mathematical exactitude we shall win the victory for ideology. We cannot say this to those who still believe the stupidities they were taught and brought up to believe. But there are times when these things can be said amongst us, sworn comrades.[2]

Party speaker at school for Party leaders,
June 1936

Unfortunately, few German churchmen were capable of setting up the kind of resistance which the earlier history of the Church has shown to be the most effective. Among the Evangelical churchmen in particular, as we have seen, the inbred qualities of obedience, loyalty and service to the State could not easily be discarded. Furthermore . . . the narrowness of the Evangelical Church's theological thinking proved inadequate to the task. The majority of churchmen retreated into a passivity which both encouraged and assisted the Nazis in their plans for persecution and subordination.[3]

Three

GOD'S LAW IS SUPREME

(How to Really Tick Off a Federal Judge)

"I don't think it's right to try and close down a doctor's legal business."

So why was I in jail this time? I had offended Federal Judge Robert Kelly in a big way, so he put me in jail, indefinitely. I had no trial, no jury, no attorney, and no opportunity to present evidence in my defense.

I was his personal political prisoner. (I ended up spending one week in custody. Nothing like good lawyers.)

"But what was your crime?" you insist. Technically, I was held "in contempt of court." The truth is, I *was* in contempt of his court—fierce contempt. Any judge who would order police to open up a death camp—an abortuary where children are murdered, including *viable* children (children seven and eight months old in their mother's womb)—should be held in contempt without apology. But more on that later.

The judge's first impression of me (and my attitude toward his injunction) was received via local television and newspaper. It just so happened that the judge was watching television and heard my bold declarations. He saw me tell a reporter his injunction was meaningless as

21

I threw it on the ground. That greased the skids for my slide into Sing-Sing.

It gets better. The night before my court hearing, I preached to a crowd of about three hundred outside the abortion mill. I was in rare form. You should have seen me. We had a blaring portable public address system. Every activist, every cop, and every member of the enemy's camp could hear me clearly. I preached my heart out. This is the gist of what I said:

"There is an injunction concerning this abortion mill. It's in Proverbs 24:11-12. 'Rescue those being led away to death; hold back those staggering toward slaughter. If you say, "But we knew nothing about this," does not he who weighs the heart perceive it? Does not he who guards your life know it? Will he not repay each person according to what he has done?'

"The Supreme Judge of the world has issued this injunction. It is irrevocable! And someday we must all appear before His judgment seat to be judged not only for what we believe, but for what we have done.

"When God judges us, what standard of right and wrong do you think He is going to use? The Supreme Court's? The U.S. Constitution? How about the Westminster Confession?

"Of course not. He is going to judge all men according to what is written in the Holy Scriptures. The Bible. The Word of God. That's it. No more, no less. The authority of God and His Word will be inescapable on that awesome day."

I had everyone's attention. People were "amening." Then I began to focus in on the godlessness of Judge Kelly's order.

"Until we get to heaven, many foolish mortals ignore, challenge, or otherwise contest the authority of God's Word. Throughout history men have come and gone who have sought to reject the authority of God's Word.

"Voltaire was a key leader in the French 'enlightenment.' He said that Christianity and the Bible would soon be extinct. Well, Voltaire is gone and the Bible is still here. In fact, after he died, his home was purchased and made into a print shop where Bibles were printed!" (The crowd was now getting even more spirited.)

I continued. "Throughout history, tyrants have arisen that have tried to usurp the authority of the Word of God. They have come, and they have gone. Hitler came, and Hitler went. Stalin came, and Stalin went. Mao came, and Mao went. But God's Word remains."

Then I really bore in on Judge Kelly.

"Now I want to tell you of another tyrant that has arisen. Unfortunately, tyrants tend to leave thousands or millions of dead in their wake. He too will leave the dead innocent in his wake. His name is Judge Robert Kelly, a federal judge who has ordered us to let babies die. He has arrogantly ordered me not to obey God's injunction, *which* commands us to rescue the innocent (Prov. 24:11, Ps. 82:2-4), but to obey his, which commands us to let the death camps operate unhindered."

By now I was thundering. (It's amazing the boldness that the anointing of the Spirit, the roar of the crowd, and the flow of adrenaline can produce. It's quite a bit different behind bars with just the anointing—no crowd, no adrenaline. Ouch!)

I continued. "We must fear our God more than we fear this judge. This injunction should be of no consequence to us, because God has already told us what to do in His Word. This judge should have done his homework. If he had, he would know that we don't obey injunctions that tell us to ignore God's injunctions. These things are not worth the paper they are written on! They might as well be toilet paper—except they have ink on them!" (Yes, I did say this. I know, it was crass. Sorry.)

"Our response to this injunction should be simple—we want to tell this judge to send this injunction back to hell where it came from!"

The crowd was inspired. I was on fire—impassioned, zealous.

And I was being listened to by the attorney for the abortion mill who got the injunction.

He was taking notes.

He read his notes to the judge the next morning in court.

I'm sure you can guess how the judge responded. He was definitely not a jolly jurist. But I'm getting ahead of myself.

The next morning, a federal marshal and a Bureau of Alcohol, Tobacco and Firearms (A.T.F.) agent arrested Reverend Pat Mahoney, Reverend Jim Evans, and myself. (I'm glad they didn't rush us with heavy arms or a tank like they have been known to do.) Actually, Pat and I had left the abortuary—the agents lured us back and then arrested us.

When we were in the holding cell, waiting to see the judge, I told the guys, "We ain't getting out'a here. He is going to put us in jail until we promise to obey his order."

They should have said, "What you mean 'we,' paleface!" They were both freed. I went to the clink. At that time, the judge was gunning for one man—me.

The federal marshal arrived to escort us from our cell into the huge federal courtroom. Tension hung in the air. After the police told the judge briefly what had happened in the street outside the abortion mill that morning, the abortion mill attorney recounted to the judge my spontaneous speech from the night before (complete with references to Hitler, Stalin, toilet paper, taking the injunction back to hell, etc.). The judge then set his glaring eyes on me and called me to the podium. In that moment, I felt as if the witnesses of heaven were watching me. By God's grace I was determined to be a prophetic witness to that judge, before God and men, angels and demons.

The following dialogue has been taken directly from the transcript of my appearance before Judge Patrick Kelly on 24 July 1991:

BY THE COURT:

Q: You are Randall Terry?

A: Yes, sir, I am.

Q: I have singled you out first in that anyone who watches television in the recent few days has watched you and heard you. I have. You are here from Operation Rescue, I take it, are you not?

A: That is correct, sir.

Q: All right. I take it you are, in fact, in charge or responsible for the organized protest of certain medical centers here in Wichita, is that right?

A: I'm certainly one of the leaders.

Q: All right. And yesterday you did receive an order from this Court that would require you to desist from the encouragement of blocking egress or ingress of the Tiller facility, did you not?

A: That is correct, sir.

Q: All right. And I have heard some comments as to your response to that; in fact, I watched you on television myself last night, so I don't need much evidence to tell me what your attitude is. But I thought what I would do today is bring the three of you here or any others that are leaders in this matter and have received this order, if for no other reason than to reason with you in what I appreciate is a rather emotional matter, but, by the same token, to have you understand, and those with you, that the order of this Court will be complied with, and without apology, without delay. And I do not intend to acquiesce in anybody who will defy an order, as I am convinced you have done to this moment.

What say you with regard to your role since you received my order?

A: Well, I too, Your Honor, in the presence of God and these witnesses say without apology that this man [the abortionist] is a child-killer, and that all of us are going to stand before the Supreme Judge of the universe, yourself included, and that His Laws are binding upon all men and all nations everywhere at all times. And that the statements that the counsel made were a little bit out of context, certainly out of order. But I'm sure that you heard me say on the TV last night that we have an injunction in the Holy Scriptures to rescue the innocent, and that if any judge, Your Honor included, should seek to tell us to not follow God's Law or not save innocent children from death, then it's null and void. That is what tyranny is, when any human authority seeks to usurp the authority of the Word of God.

Q: If I understand it then, Mr. Terry, what you're saying is if you leave here today and return to the Tiller facility, you would take up again with the encouragement of doing that which you deem necessary to obstruct egress or ingress of either Dr. Tiller or his staff or patients, is that correct?

A: Before I answer that, Your Honor—yes, that is correct, but there is something that I would request at some juncture.

Q: You have told me enough, Mr. Terry. Your answer tells me that you do intend to defy the order that was handed to you yesterday for whatever reasons that are yours.

A: Your Honor, the doctor in question kills children, 7th and 8th month viable children.

Q: Let me say that we are dealing with this Court and this Court's order.

A: Your court ordered officers and us to defend the clinic where babies that are viable will be killed.

Q: I intended to see that the order of this Court is complied with, as are the laws of this country complied with, and you have received a lawful order that requires compliance with the laws of this country, and you will not impair the rights of others. And inasmuch as you have indicated to me of your intentions to continue with that defiance, I find your conduct, your answer, in contempt of my order of yesterday, and I don't believe it's necessary we have any further hearing or any further notice or any further warning.

As a consequence, I order you to the custody of the United States Marshal, and you will be held in custody, Mr. Terry, until such time as you elect to purge yourself from your defiance of this order, which is to say until such time as you're ready to say to me that you're ready to comply with the laws of this country and the laws of this order, which are clear and have been handed to you and which you fully understand. Do you understand?

A: I believe that you're inaccurate in your assessment of the laws of this country, but that is an issue for appeal.

THE COURT: Marshal, would you take him into custody?

Bye-bye, Mr. American Pie

And so I was escorted to jail as a federal prisoner.

What do you think? Was I wrong? Did I deserve to sit in jail because I violated a judge's "lawful order"?

Should I have obeyed the judge and let babies die unprotected? Or should I have obeyed God's Law, believing (as I do) that God's Law is higher than man's law?

Lip Service, Inc.

Most Christians today pay lip service to the concept of "Higher Law." They acknowledge that God's Law is higher than man's law. Even those who are the most rabidly against Operation Rescue, even those who say we should always obey the law of man, celebrate the Fourth of July. (So much for consistency.)

I'll bet that most Christians in America have never stopped to seriously meditate on "The Fourth of July," its biblical and philosophical underpinnings, and what the Declaration of Independence meant for the signers.

It meant the signers were breaking the law.

In fact, it meant they were guilty of treason.

It meant they were prepared to go to war for the freedoms we take for granted.

It meant that real men fired real bullets at other real men who shed real blood, died excruciating, real deaths, and left behind real grieving widows and orphans on both sides of the war.

The American Revolution was not a debate about Romans 13 nor a civics lesson on freedom. It was a war for freedom dedicated to the proposition that all men are endowed by their Creator with certain inalienable rights; it was a war founded on a belief in Higher Law.

Tragically, while most Christians pay lip service to "Higher Law," they do not possess a concrete or even modest conviction or understanding of Higher Law.

Those Christians who argue against Operation Rescue or smuggling Bibles into China or praying at high-school graduations on the basis of Romans 13 have foolishly turned the Bible on its head. They have made God's Word subservient to man's evil law—in the name of Romans 13. In the name of the Bible, they subjugate the Bible to pagans. Unfortunately, those "law and order" Christians have not looked at the whole Bible, nor rightly divided the Word of Truth. Let's take a little closer look at Romans 13:1-5:

> Let every person be in subjection to the governing authorities. For there is no authority except from God, and those which exist are established by God. Therefore he who resists authority has opposed the ordinance of God; and they who have opposed will receive condemnation upon themselves. For rulers are not a cause of fear for good behavior, but for evil. Do you want to have no fear of authority? Do what is good and you will have praise from the same; for it is a minister of God to you for good. But if you do what is evil, be afraid; for it does not bear the sword for nothing; for it is a minister of God, an avenger who brings wrath upon the one who practices evil.

> Wherefore it is necessary to be in subjection, not only
> because of wrath, but also for conscience' sake.

Please note that God ordained government to punish wicked doers and to praise the righteous. Question: What do we do when the government rejects its *God-ordained duty* and does the exact opposite—praising and protecting the wicked, while punishing and persecuting the righteous? This passage does not deal with that dilemma.

I believe the apostle Peter answered the question most succinctly when he said, "We must obey God rather than men" (Acts 5:29). Again and again we see in the Scriptures that when God's Law and man's law conflict, the saints of God must obey God. Consider the Hebrew midwives (Exod. 1:15-21); Moses' parents (Exod. 1:22-2:5; Heb. 11:23); Rahab the Harlot—who also lied (Josh. 2; Heb. 11:31); Daniel (Dan. 6); the three Hebrew children (Dan. 3); the wise men (Matt. 2:1-12); the disciples who smuggled Paul over a wall in a basket (Acts 9:23-25; 2 Cor. 11:32-33); and the angel who led Peter in a jail break (Acts 12:5-10), just to give a quick overview.

Also note that the saints of God "broke the law" not only when they were commanded to do evil, *but when they were commanded to not do good.* "Don't pray!" Daniel was told. "Don't preach," the apostles were told. Christians nowadays are told, "Don't rescue babies"; "Don't smuggle Bibles"; "Don't preach about political matters in your church"; "Don't pray at school commencements."

We need to do some serious studying and thinking and do it *fast.* The conflict between God's Law and man's law is not only in the realms I've mentioned. The battle is intensifying in America on a multitude of fronts. The pagans are using the law to slowly crush biblical morality and justice on all fronts. The God-haters are using the law to harass and intimidate families and churches who believe and practice the teachings of the Bible. "Children's rights" lunatics are using the law to persecute parents who spank their children. The statists are slowly using man's law to obtain control over what pastors preach and whom they hire.

First Principle—God Rules

We've got to accept this simple principle, friend: God rules. His Law is supreme. And He requires all men in all nations at all times to obey His laws. And when His Law and man's law conflict, His Law is the unquestionable authority. Man's law at that point is unrighteous tyranny.

Some Questions

For those who doubt this conclusion, please consider these questions:

Whose law is eternal—God's or man's?

Can God's Law be rescinded, revised, or improved?

Does God hold His Law or man's law to be higher when the two are in conflict?

Does God want His people to obey His Law or man's when the two are in conflict?

Does God hold all rulers in all nations—including non-Christians—accountable to His Law, or are the lost free to do what they want?

If the lost are free to do as they please, to what standard will God hold them accountable? By what standard will He judge them? How can the Holy Spirit convict them of sin if the measure of sin (the Law) has been removed?

Friend, we need to forever settle in our minds and hearts the supremacy of God's Law. While we quibble over what place we think the Bible should have in culture and law, our enemies know exactly where they want the Bible.

Our Enemies' Vision for the Bible

Our enemies want the complete eradication of Christianity and biblical principles from our public symbols, our schools, our city, county, state, and federal governments, etc.

The secular Humanist elite preach "tolerance," but they are absolutely intolerant of a God-centered, Bible-based view of law and culture. They want the influence of the Law of God eradicated from this nation (except, of course, the part in Romans 13 that the pietists wrongly believe calls them to submit to the pagan government's every demand—rebels in power love to wave Romans 13 in front of Christians).

The pagan elite and Bible-phobes boldly march forward, trying to stamp out biblical Christianity, while we timidly speak of a "Judeo-Christian ethic," "pluralism," and "tolerance."

I believe that those Christian leaders, teachers, and pastors who side with man's law above God's Law are unwitting collaborators with the enemy for America's demise. They might mean well—they might be sincere—but they are sincerely deceived and sincerely deceiving. Look in my book, *Accessory To Murder*, to see how men like Norman Geisler, John MacArthur, and Bill Gothard are making the same mistakes that the German clergy made in the 1930s.

Just for example, in 1989, Norman Giesler and I had an impromptu, face-to-face debate about higher law. I asked him this question "If you (Norman) were a Soviet pastor fleeing from Joseph Stalin, and Stalin intended to kill you, if I took you in illegally, and hid you, would I be wrong?" He schocked me and everyone else who was listening when he answered without hestatation, "Yes."

Imagine! A Christian author, supposedly an intelligent Bible-based thinker, is telling me it would be wrong to shelter a Christian pastor who was fleeing for his life from a murderous communist dictator! What have we come to?

Our Vision of the Bible

Let us be just as bold—no, more bold—than God's enemies. Not only is God's Law above man's law, but it must undergird man's law. For man's law to be legitimate, it must be founded on biblical law.

We want our nation and all its institutions to be self-consciously built on the laws and principles of God's Word. Any other foundation will crumble. God's Law is over all human authority. And God's Law is the only unchanging, transcendent law from heaven, the only set of moral absolutes upon which human authority can rest.

Those clergy and Christian leaders who insist that we not enter the cultural fray with the Ten Commandments as our spoken foundation are misguided, and they are leading the church astray. (We will discuss this further in chapter 7 on "The Battle of Allegiances.")

"Religion and Politics Don't Mix"—Satan

Not only are many Christian leaders unsure of the supremacy of God's Law over man's law, not only are they confused about biblical law being the foundation of man's law, but they question whether or not we should even discuss human law in connection with biblical law. They feel it's out of bounds for us.

The antichrists in power like nothing better than when pastors proclaim hell's party lines: "Religion and politics don't mix," and "Don't bring politics in the church," and "We live in a pluralistic society, so we can't bring our Christian convictions into politics." This is foolishness, a deception from hell. The rebels in power pronounce their rebellion against God, and we so much as tell them this is their right, that God accepts their "pluralistic" rebellion. But God warns them: "Serve the Lord with fear, and rejoice with trembling. Kiss the Son, lest he be angry, and ye perish from the way" (Ps. 2:11-12).

Equal Time with Hell

Yet another attempt at compromise that many Christian leaders have come up with at first seems reasonable, but is rotten to the core. It goes like this: "We just want equal time."

Wrong! We don't want "equal time" with baby-killers, condom pushers, New Agers, one-worlders, and sodomite recruiters. We do not want them to have any access to public schools. We won't tolerate their having a single minute to expose our children or anyone else's children to their godless agenda. Planned Parenthood, Queer Nation, and their cohorts from hell have no right to give the time of day to children in school—much less try and fill their unsuspecting minds with filth. We don't want equal time, because we want them to have *no time.*

We will not put the flawless, eternal Word of God on the same par with godless laws, or the ungodly lies of men and demons. God's Law is supreme and will abide forever. Man's rebellious thoughts are as chaff for the fire.

Intolerance Is a Beautiful Thang

In the light of God's holy, flawless, unchanging eternal Word, we have a duty to be intolerant of the pagan world agenda. They often accuse us of being intolerant. We should wear this intended insult as a badge of honor.

Consider a few biblical figures:

• David was intolerant of Goliath (1 Sam. 17).

• The prophet Elijah was intolerant of Jezebel (1 Kings 18, 21).

• The apostle Paul was intolerant of books on witchcraft—the books were burned! (How's *that* for being politically incorrect! See Acts 19:19.)

Or let's consider some recent historical figures who were intolerant—including men and women the so-called liberals cherish.

• Thomas Jefferson was intolerant of King George III.

• George Washington was intolerant of British troops.

• Frederick Douglass and Harriet Tubman were intolerant of slavery.

• Susan B. Anthony—a pro-life suffragette—was intolerant of only men voting.

• Lech Walesa is intolerant of communism.

• And Mother Teresa is intolerant of abortion.

Intolerance *is* a beautiful thing!

Long Live Righteous Intolerance!

In the book of Revelations, Jesus rebuked the church of *Thyatira* because "you tolerate the woman Jezebel, who calls herself a prophetess, and she teaches and leads my bond-servants astray, so that they commit acts of immorality and eat things sacrificed to idols." (Rev. 2:20)

So please, don't waver. Your love for God and His Word should make you intolerant of abominations and perversions. We must reach out in mercy to those who are trapped in sin; we must offer the grace of God to His enemies, but we are not called to shower "mush love" on those who are knowingly, deliberately leading people astray. We must warn the enemies' leaders of the coming judgment of God and encourage them to repent and turn to Christ. But we must also denounce their agenda and fearlessly rebuke their paganism, especially in public settings. Your allegiance to the King of the Universe should make you intolerant of the prophets of Baal—the leaders and the agenda of the rebels of our day. In fact, you may want to read 1 Kings 18 to see the contempt God's prophets have for Baal's prophets. The false prophets were proclaiming lies. Elijah was prophesying God's Word. Elijah *mocked* them.

Why? Because Elijah knew the only true God and had received His Word. The prophets of Baal were following deceptive demons, prophesying lies, and leading the people astray. Elijah did not dignify their pagan deity, pagan ideas, and pagan immorality by showing pluralistic respect for what he knew was a hellish lie.

God's Law is supreme. Heaven and earth will pass away, but God's Word will not. And if the culture is going to survive, every power base must be rebuilt on the bedrock of God's Law. We cannot compromise with the prophets of Baal. We cannot appease those who are dedicated to our demise.

By its decision to carry out the political and moral cleansing of our public life. . . .The national Government sees in both Christian denominations the most important factor for the maintenance of our society.[1]

Adolf Hitler, March 1933
(In his first statement to the new Reichstag)

The curriculum of all categories in our schools has already been so far reformed in an anti-Christian and anti-Jewish spirit that the generation which is growing up will be protected from the black swindle (clergy).[2]

Alfred Rosenberg, November 1938

Four

666, ANYONE?

(Pick a Date! Any Date!)

"I think things are going to get even worse before the Lord returns."

They just don't give up. The rapture date-setters and the Antichrist-namers never seem to skip a beat, in spite of how many times they've been wrong. In recent times, the Antichrist was assuredly Henry Kissinger (Jewish!); then Jimmy Carter (a *professing* believer—hmmm); then Mikhail Gorbachev (he had that thing on his head); then Sadaam Hussein (if he attacked Israel the trumpet would sound). I wonder who their next victim will be. I'm taking bets on Boris Yeltsin or Bill Clinton. (Horror, there's an idea.)

And, of course, there was the best seller, *88 Reasons Why the Rapture Will Be in 1988.* I wanted to write the sequel, *88 Reasons Why It Wasn't.* I don't think many publishers would have been interested.

Now the *insane* book, by Harold Camping, 1994, is a best seller (as of the spring of 1993). This book will also be wrong. "How can you be so sure?" you may ask. Well, every time, since the Ascension of Christ, some well–meaning (or deceived) Christian has defied Christ's words and tried to pick a date, they've been wrong. The date-setters are batting 1000 percent at being wrong.

So . . . *I predict 1995!* (The whole year! Those reading after 1995, don't smirk. Just beware of the next date-setter.)

The truth be known, I cut my teeth spiritually around people (and tapes and books) that proved to me—with lots of Bible verses—that because Israel had again become a political state in 1948, and because vultures were laying two eggs instead of one in the Middle East, and because the Soviets' military hardware could be burned like coal for $3^{1/2}$ years, and because someone was developing a microchip to put in people's foreheads or hands so we could be a cashless society, and because our credit cards had a hologram, and because "The Beast" (a computer in Belgium) was working for the revived Roman Empire, and . . . and . . . *and* . . . the secret rapture of the Church was going to be any minute.

It was probably useless to plan to be in Russia to preach the gospel during the 1980 Olympics because we would be raptured by then. *Certainly*, we would be whisked away before 1981. Of course, 1981 came and went, as did 1984, as did 1988, as did the war with Iraq. The date-setters and vulture-watchers had substantial vulture egg on their faces. The late, great, planet earth is still here! (It was undoubtedly a greater earth for those who had a good hunk of change in their pockets from book royalties—something an author never scoffs at!)

It would be bad enough if the date-setters simply deluded themselves with *New York Times*-CNN headlines. But it's worse than that. Not only don't they fight to stop America's moral collapse, they sometimes seem to *rejoice* in it.

America Is Dying. Hallelujah! Maranatha!

For the secret rapture watchers, the rapid collapse of America's families and the rampant immorality we see all around us are signs that we are fast approaching the end of time. Like a numbing theological narcotic that keeps people in their rapture-watching armchairs is the belief that the more corrupt America becomes, the more certain we can be that the rapture is any second. "Let it rot, baby! We're going up!"

The worse it gets, the better. The prevailing wickedness of the hour is a welcome confirmation for the prophets of escapism. "More Christians are being oppressed! The divorce rate is skyrocketing! Homosexuals want to take over! Glory to God, the end is near! Jesus must be coming any second!" This latter part is shrieked in increasingly shrill tones.

Explain to the oppressed Christians in China or in the former Soviet Union—who have suffered for decades—that the minor persecution of American Christians is the prelude to Armageddon. What a joke.

Eschatologis Vomitus

Well, forgive me for being blunt, but I just don't buy it anymore. I am sick of date-setting and antichrist-watching. I'm sick of the unhealthy distraction it is to Christians. I'm sick of it ripping their hearts out.

Now, please don't misunderstand me. I believe the Scriptures. The Bible clearly teaches of the bodily return of the Lord Jesus (Acts 1:11), the blessed hope (Titus 2:13). It will be a glorious event. And I believe His return may happen today, or tomorrow. We should live to please Him, so that if He appears, we will not be ashamed before Him at His coming (1 John 2:28). We should also live in a way that if He doesn't come for two thousand more years, we will not deliver a cursed nation to our great-great-grandchildren. We want to leave a legacy of righteousness and courage for our grandchildren, not escapism and cowardice.

Frankly, it wouldn't surprise me if the Second Coming *was* two thousand years from now. (Don't close the book yet! I'm not a heretic!)

The Long Last Days

"But what about the signs?" some will ask. "We're in the last days!"

Yes, we are in the last days. We've been in the last days since the day of Pentecost. On the day of Pentecost, when the Holy Spirit was poured out with incredible power, signs, and wonders, commencing with the one hundred and twenty disciples speaking in other tongues, Peter stood up and declared we were in the last days. He quoted Joel 2:28-32:

> For these men are not drunk, as you suppose, for it is only the third hour of the day; but this is what was spoken through the prophet Joel: "And it shall be in the last days, God says, that I will pour forth of my Spirit upon all mankind, and your sons and your daughters shall prophesy, and your young men shall see visions, and your old men shall dream dreams; even upon my bond slaves, both men and women, I will, in those days, pour out my Spirit; and they shall prophesy. And I will grant wonders in the sky above and signs on the earth beneath, blood, and fire, and vapor of smoke. The sun shall be turned into darkness and the moon into blood, before the great and glorious day of the Lord shall come. And, it shall be that everyone who calls on the name of the Lord shall be saved.'" (Acts 2:15-21)

"But the Signs!"

Consider this. The Lord's first advent was prophesied *extensively* in the Old Testament. If the religious leaders of Jesus' day—the Scribes, the Pharisees, the theologians, the watchers of the signs—could not "discern the times," if they couldn't see the Messiah's coming when it was right under their noses, then what makes us so cocksure that we can predict His second coming with such pinpoint accuracy? It is blatant arrogance on our part.

In fact, when we pick dates we fly in the face of the Scriptures. Jesus clearly stated, "No man knows the day or hour" (Matt. 24:36). (But Harold Camping says we can know the month and the year—hmmm.)

So why do we pick dates?

Hell's Bells and Whistles

Frankly, I believe date-setting is probably a distraction and a deception from hell. Well-meaning, overzealous men and women have fallen into the enemy's snare. Obviously, they've all been wrong. And for the Christians over the centuries who have built their lives or altered their plans based on these erroneous predictions—they have thrown away months, years, perhaps decades of their lives. For example, I wonder in recent times how many Christian men had a yearning to be a congressman or a judge, but abandoned the dream early on because "Jesus is coming any second." This nonsense of date-setting has robbed the church and the culture.

Saints who are unhealthily preoccupied with the Lord's coming generally aren't obeying the parabolic command to "occupy till I come" (Luke 19:13).

Rotten Fruit

Jesus said, "A tree is known by its fruit" (Matt. 12:33). The fruit of date-setting, second coming star-watchers, and antichrist pickers has been utterly disastrous. Whether Christians sell all they have and cloister on a mountaintop waiting for the trumpet blast, or whether they run up big credit card bills to leave the antichrist while they cloister in their safe, cozy, and culturally irrelevant churches, the result is the same. They are useless in the great cultural battles for biblical justice and righteousness.

What if, rather than being deluded into accepting America's moral collapse as our divine destiny, a "sign of the times," the millions and millions of Christians who were unhealthily preoccupied with the rapture for the past seventy years had been the salt of the earth and fought against baby-killers, pornographers, condom-pushers, messianic statists, and sodomite evangelists? We wouldn't be in the mess we are in now!

We have been deceived by Satan himself into surrendering the greatest nation in the history of the world (save ancient Israel) to pagan elitists—and we've done so

believing that God had destined this nation to moral collapse, that he destined the church for defeat! We've foolishly believed that God was pleased with us for standing
idly by while a nation sank into the bowels of hell, because we were watching eternal drama play out. God
deliver us from the theology of escapism.

Yes, the Lord will return. Yes, His coming is the blessed
hope. Yes, we should pray with John the Beloved, "Even
so, come, Lord Jesus" (Rev. 22:20c). But I believe the
American churches' excessive preoccupation with the
Lord's return is out of balance, unbiblical, and has led us
into a retreatist, escapist mentality. Compare how much
of the Bible is devoted to how we should live here and
now, to how little of the Bible is devoted to eschatology
(the study of end times).

Why Polish Brass on a Sinking Ship?

As I stated earlier, the fruit of the date-setting "any
second rapture" crowd has been absolutely disastrous.
Literally millions of American Christians—perhaps yourself included—are content to let America slide into moral
anarchy because they think it's God's will for wickedness
to flourish before the Lord returns. It's a sign of the times!
Jesus is going to come any second.

And besides, if Jesus is going to come tomorrow, why
be involved in the moral issues of today? Or to quote a
famous radio Bible teacher, "Why polish brass on a sink-
ing ship?"

If you are a rapture date-setter, I have this question
for you: What if America's moral disintegration has absolutely nothing to do with the Lord's return? What if the
mockery of righteousness has nothing to do with Matthew 24, but everything to do with Matthew 5? "If the
salt have lost his savor, wherewith shall it be salted? it is
thenceforth *good for nothing*, but to be cast out, and to be
trodden under foot of men" (Matt. 5:13, emphasis added).
The *Living New Testament* says the salt is "worthless"!
That's what many Christians have become—*worthless*.

I believe the rise of persecution against Christians, the mockery of Christianity, and the spurning of Christian principles in America have nothing to do with the Lord's return. We and our most sacred principles are mocked and trampled underfoot *because we are the salt that lost its savor.* Our own selfishness, laziness, bless-me-club Christianity, coupled with our detachment from and irrelevance in this culture have gotten us in this mess. Our own folly has made us a prey to the jaws of tyranny. To use the Lord's words, we are good for nothing. And as He promised, we are being trampled under foot of men.

Cast Off the Shackles

I believe we must challenge the date-setting preoccupation in the church because of the damage done to the church and the nation. I also believe the great escape mentality has helped bring us to the brink of destruction. Because of the incredible amount of ground we have lost since the early 1900s, we are now entrenched in a life and death struggle for our own survival and for the survival of America as a free nation. We've been *clearly losing* since the early 1960s. To top it off, most Christians don't have a clue how to fight, where to fight, who to fight, when to fight, and most importantly, *why* to fight.

I recently talked with an "expert prophecy teacher" who insisted that he could still be an "activist" while being pre-occupied with the rapture. (It was a very polite and amiable conversation.) I told him, "Perhaps you can live with that apparent schizophrenia, but the average person in the pew cannot. Some of the hugest evangelical churches in America that are unhealthily preoccupied with the Lord's return have little or no influence in the power bases of their communities (the schools, media, universities, the police force, the judiciary, the medicines, the arts, etc.). They have the manpower to take back the 'power bases,' but instead they're all worked up about the latest *New York Times* headline about Israel or Sadaam Hussein."

A woman sitting by and listening in suddenly spoke

up, expressing her deep frustration. "Every time I go to my church and try and get them involved, people tell me 'the Lord is coming any time now, and we don't need to worry about changing the world.'" The prophecy expert ignored her anecdotal evidence and my arguments.

Destined to Lose

Moreover, many Christians believe we are destined to be defeated. Before the Lord's return, society will have decayed so completely that it will be impossible to reform it. There's no way we can win—"until that trumpet blast." For now, well there's not much we can do. So why bother? The average Christian simply isn't going to get in a battle he isn't going to win. I know a few people declare, "We must remain faithful till the end." But not many Christians will join the fight if the battle cry is "We're going to get slaughtered, God has destined us to lose, but we're called to be faithful! Let's see who can bang their head against the wall the longest!"

Forget the Alamo!

Another tragic side effect of "rapture fever" is amnesia. We forget. We forget from whence we've fallen as a nation. We forget what great freedom and justice our spiritual forefathers fought for, and sometimes died for. And perhaps more tragically, we forget our responsibility to our children, grandchildren, and our great-grandchildren. Many Christians have little or no sense of compelling duty for their yet unborn children and grandchildren. Why? Because they think the end of the world will be here before their grandchildren or great-grandchildren are.

What Dread Lies Ahead?

Question: Given our current direction, what will this nation look like one hundred years from now if the Lord *doesn't* return? What horrifying barbarisms will be commonplace because we chose not to stand and fight when we could have turned the tide?

We have foolishly, selfishly spent our children's future freedom for our own current comfort and ease. Our children may pay a horrifying price for the freedom to bear children, to raise children as they see fit, and to preach the whole counsel of God (i.e., "Sodomy is an abomination!"—perfect words for a hate crime).

Our children's money may be valueless; our daughters may be drafted to fight and die in war (after being raped by their captors); besides importing clothes, shoes, and toys from China, we may also import forced sterilization and forced abortion; school systems may be forced to indoctrinate children into the sodomite agenda; social services may take children from parents who are too religious or who spank their children.

For those who think these words the predictions of a madman, consider this: In 1959 (the year I was born), it would have been inconceivable to the average American that we would have thirty-five million children murdered by abortion (as of 1993); homosexuals marching in the street demanding the right to be married; tax money paying for a crucifix floating in a jar of urine; or a Hollywood movie titled *"The Last Temptation"* that blasphemes Christ. It would have been inconceivable that one day it would be illegal for a public school teacher to recite the Lord's Prayer or the 23rd Psalm, but permissible for that same teacher to tell our children where to get abortions or condoms without our consent or knowledge.

What is common today was unthinkable one generation ago.

Question: What is unthinkable today that will be commonplace tomorrow? We have a lot shorter distance to go from here to forced abortion or sodomite marriages than the distance from "Ozzie and Harriet" to Ozzy Osborne and Madonna. God open our eyes to what looms on the future's horizon!

In the Year 2525

But millions of American Christians aren't burdened about their offsprings' future. The only dark spot they see on the horizon is Armageddon. And for them that is a bright spot! So why strive to achieve righteousness and justice in the judiciary, politics, the medicines, schools, universities or the media, for future generations? Why be burdened for our offspring and their offspring? We'll be long gone!

What grieves me so deeply is that it doesn't have to be this way. The pagans don't have an irrevocable destiny to run this country into hell. They are not invincible. American Christians have the manpower and the money to take back the power bases. Just consider the tens of millions of professing Christians, and the *billions* we spend on buildings, Crystal Cathedrals, and entertainment. We have the numbers and money, but we don't have the vision, the passion, or the sense of duty before God to take the Lordship of Christ in every citadel of authority.

If the enemy continues to seduce us to let America perish, and we continue to squander our children's freedom, future generations throughout the world will hold us in harsh contempt. Our great-grandchildren will curse this generation of Christians for our cowardice and escapist mentality. But I'm sure some Christian author or teacher will try to tickle itching ears in their day telling them that *they* are the terminal generation. ("This time we're *really* sure. Vultures are laying *three* eggs!")

Confess, Randall!

So, you may be wondering, what is my eschatology? I'm a pan-millenialist—with post-millenial tendencies. I believe it's all going to pan out in the end. And I assure you, I'm right. It all will pan out in the end! I know that sounds like a cop-out, but it's not. Let me put more flesh on the bones.

I believe righteousness is a greater force than wickedness (Eph. 6:10-17).

I believe we are the light of the world (Matt. 5:14).

I believe that although gross darkness is on the peoples, that the glory of the Lord will shine on us and ultimately cover the earth (see Isaiah 60).

I believe light is greater than darkness, and that darkness cannot overcome light (John 1:5).

I believe "greater is He who is in you than he who is in the world" (1 John 4:4).

When we are doing what we should be doing, with God's anointing, the wicked cannot prevail against us.

I believe Jesus will build His church, and the gates of hell will not prevail against it (see Matthew 16:18). *Gates are for defense.* When the church of God is on the offensive, walking in holiness and obedience, the "gates of hell," protecting the interests of hell, cannot withstand us. Child-killers, earth-worshippers, and pornographers are no match for an obedient, Holy Spirit-animated church.

I believe the earth is the Lord's and the fullness thereof, not the devil's (Ps. 24:1a).

I believe Jesus was manifested to destroy the works of the devil (1 John 3:8). If we are conformed to His image (Rom. 8:29), we will also destroy the works of the devil. I believe we can rebuild the ancient ruins and raise up the age-old foundations of righteousness (see Isaiah 58:6-12 and Isaiah 61:1-6).

I believe that the Kingdom of God is like a grain of mustard seed, which grows into a plant that dominates the whole garden (Luke 13:18-19).

I believe Christ is the Rock cut without hands who smashes the idol's feet and slowly fills the earth (Dan. 2:45).

I believe all authority, in heaven *and earth,* is given to Christ now (Matt. 28:18).

I believe He is the King of kings and Lord of lords *now* (see 1 Timothy 6:15). He is the boss.

I believe all kings, princes, and judges are duty bound

to obey Him *now*, lest He destroy them in His wrath (see Psalm 2).

I believe Jesus is returning for a glorious church—without spot or wrinkle (Eph. 5:27)—not some beaten down church whimpering in the corner until Jesus comes!

The parable said, "Occupy till I come," not "hide out till I come" (Luke 19:13).

Finally (and this is for the true eschatological student), I believe most of Matthew 24 and book of Revelation are history.

This is a quick (and not comprehensive) view of my eschatology.

With all this said, let me make something perfectly clear: I will gladly and joyfully work alongside any trinitarian Christian, but if I had my druthers, I would rather serve with an (inconsistent) activist-premillenialist than an armchair post-millenialist.

The Antichrist Who Isn't

Finally, the Bible does not say there will be one special antichrist. John said, "Little children, it is the last time: and as ye have heard that antichrist shall come, even *now there are many antichrists*; whereby we know that it is the last time" (1 John 2:18, emphasis added). That's right. *Many* antichrists. "Who is the liar but he who denies that Jesus is the Christ? He is antichrist, that denies the Father and the Son" (1 John 2:22). Anyone who denies that Jesus is the Christ is an antichrist.

I understand that the antichrist-watchers believe the "man of sin" of 2 Thessalonians 2:3 and the "Beast" of Revelation 13 is *the* Antichrist. However, this is a strained, unbiblical leap of logic.

Our preoccupation with an antichrist is an unhealthy, sinister distraction. Daniel wrote, "The people who know their God will display strength and take action" (Dan. 11:32)—not "those who know their antichrists." Christians who are supposed to be looking for Christ's glorious appearing are instead looking for an antichrist.

Please, friend, take an honest look at the fruit of the date-setting, antichrist-watching, we're-destined-to-get-our-butts-kicked theology in the church; look at what it has done to America. It should give you pause, and at least make you very suspicious of the current or next wave of date-setters.

Yes, the trumpet will sound, and Jesus will return in great power and glory to judge the quick and the dead. It could happen today. It might not happen for two thousand years. Just in case He decides to wait for the "restoration of all things" (Acts 3:21b), let's get busy taking ground from the enemy's hands for His kingdom.

I promise you that, if I wished to, I could destroy the Church in a few years; it is hollow and rotten and false through and through. One push and the whole structure would collapse. We should trap the priests by their notorious greed and self-indulgence. We shall thus be able to settle everything with them in perfect peace and harmony. I shall give them a few years' reprieve. Why should we quarrel? They will swallow anything in order to keep their material advantages. Matters will never come to a head. They will recognize a firm will, and we need only show them once or twice who is the master. Then they will know which way the wind blows. They are no fools. The Church was something really big. Now we are its heirs. We, too, are the Church. Its day has gone.[1]

Adolf Hitler

[The] Nazi State pursued a completely single-minded policy—to drive the Churches out of political life. Many evangelical pastors argued that the Nazi Party's drastic limitations of Church activities were to be regarded, not as a defeat, but rather as a liberation from a dangerous over-extension of ecclesiastical influence into the political arena.[2]

THE IDOL
OF REPUTATION

**(Are You Nicer Than Jesus? Just Don't Speak
the Whole Word of God!)**

*"I just wish you could do things a little different. I mean,
you read about it in the paper. I wish you could do it in a way
that doesn't give Christians a bad name . . ."*

I don't know how I do it, but I consistently bring out
the worst in people. People I don't even know hate me.
Newspaper columnists who have never met me write
against me. Television commentators I've never had a
minute with rail against me. (And I'm a likable guy!)

I go to speak in churches all over the country, and I'm
met by frothing, screaming, pro-abortion and/or homosexual activists. One time in Philadelphia the "activists
from hell" gathered at the entrance of a church parking
lot and threw condoms at our people as they entered. The
police came and, in preparing to arrest the protesters, put
rubber gloves on (in case the homosexuals had AIDS).
When the lesbian/homosexual/pro-abortion activists saw
the police putting on the rubber gloves, they yelled out,
"Oh boy! We're gonna have some 'fisting' tonight!" These
are the nice people who want you to accept their "alternative lifestyle." God save those poor lost souls.

51

Another time I was scheduled to speak at the University of San Francisco. (Yes, I knew this was a dumb move from the beginning. "Thanks" to my hosts!) About sixty Christians got inside, then the homosexuals surrounded the entryway, then the entire building. They kicked in a plate glass window, kicked a door off its hinges, refused entrance to those who wanted to get in, and made such raucous and violent threats that the police forced us to cancel the meeting. Our people had to escort each other to their cars. However, the police did not arrest *any of the sodomites.*

The Idol of Our Reputation

Okay, I'll be honest. There are times I'm encouraged when our enemies come out. It strengthens me because it reminds me that I'm on the right track. But there are times when unjust or unfounded criticism bothers me— especially from Christians—and I want to defend myself. But I learned a long time ago that the preservation of my reputation is of very little consequence to God.

Before I go any further, let me bring some balance. St. Paul wrote that if someone was to be an elder "he must have a good report from them which are without; lest he fall into reproach and the snare of the devil" (1 Tim. 3:7). And so, having a good name and a good reputation for righteous living are noble goals. "A good name is rather to be chosen than great riches" (Prov. 22:1).

But let's face it, for many of us having a good reputation has become something of an idol. What we desire is not a "good reputation" according to biblical terms. We want a good reputation *on this world's terms.* We dread the thought of looking too radical, of sounding too controversial, of doing or saying anything that would upset our neighbors, co-workers, or family members; we dread the thought of tarnishing our precious image.

Most Christians tend to refuse to take strong *public* action on a controversial issue. You would never catch them taking a public stand against child-killing, sodomy, school condom giveaways, or intrusion by "social services" into families' lives. They wouldn't want to appear at a prayerful protest with a bunch of radicals. Even worse, many Christians refuse to even *say* what they believe to relatives, fellow employees, neighbors, or even fellow Christians, for fear of displeasing them. When an opportunity presents itself, or duty cries for a simple verbal response, millions of Christians are deafeningly silent when they should be professing God's Word.

Herein lies the problem. When the dear old brother said to me that he didn't want Christians to have a bad name, he wasn't referring to a bad name because of sin, he was talking about a bad name because of zeal for righteousness. It was said of Christ, ". . . .The zeal of thine house hath eaten me up" (John 2:17).

As Christians we must believe our Lord's words and follow His example. As we will see, that might mean we will be heroes, or we may be villains.

Jesus: They Loved Him, They Despised Him

Consider Jesus' example. At times the crowds thronged around Him and exciting reports about Him spread across the country. For example:

Matthew 9:28-31: "And when he was come into the house, the blind men came to him: and Jesus saith unto them, Believe ye that I am able to do this? They said unto him, Yea, Lord. Then touched he their eyes, saying, According to your faith be it unto you. And their eyes were opened; and Jesus straitly charged them, saying, See *that* no man know it. **But they, when they were departed, spread abroad his fame in all that country.**" (emphasis added)

Mark 1:26-28: "And when the unclean spirit had torn him, and cried with a loud voice, he came out of him. And they were all amazed, insomuch that they questioned among themselves, saying, What thing is this? what new doctrine is this? for with authority commandeth he even the unclean spirits, and they do obey him. **And immedi-**

ately his fame spread abroad throughout all the region round about Galilee." (emphasis added)

Luke 5:15: "But so much the more went there a fame abroad of him: and great multitudes came together to hear, and to be healed by him of their infirmities." (emphasis added)

Jesus became famous. The multitudes sang His praises. The talk in the coffee shops was great. The editorials were positive. The disciples were basking in the attention they experienced from being close to Jesus, and it was definitely going to their heads. "Let one of us sit at your right hand and the other at your left in your glory" (Mark 10:37). Perhaps they thought, "This discipleship stuff is awesome! If this is what it means to be a disciple, I can handle it! Yo, Jesus, count me in!"

However, Jesus' popularity did not extend to all quarters. He wasn't making everybody happy. When He taught the multitudes, the malcontent maligned Him, saying, "He deceives the people" (John 7:12). When He cast out devils, certain leaders blasphemed Him, saying, "It is only by Beelzebub, the prince of demons, that this fellow drives out demons" (Matt. 12:24). When He healed the sick, the nay-sayers berated Him, saying, "This man is not from God, for He does not keep the Sabbath" (John 9:14-16). When He confronted the evil, the hypocrites accused Him, saying, "You are demon-possessed" (John 7:19-20). When He stood innocent, silent as a lamb, his enemies and the multitude condemned Him, saying, "Crucify Him! Crucify Him!" (Mark 15:12-14). When He bled and died in their place, the conspirators mocked Him, saying, "He saved others; let Him save Himself if He is the Christ of God, the Chosen One. . . . If You are the king of the Jews, save Yourself" (Luke 23:34-37).

Jesus, Me? This Isn't What I Hoped For

The apostles quickly learned that they would have a mixed review at best in this world. At times, eager inquirers clamored to be near enough for their shadows to fall on them. At other times, their shadows were extinguished in a dark jail cell. The unhappy locals screamed, "These men who have upset the world have come here also" (Acts 17:6). In Ephesus, the local idol merchants created a mob scene that could have cost Paul his life had the disciples not intervened (see Acts 19:23-41).

And lest you think these injustices and false accusations were only for Christ and the apostles, think again. "The disciple is not above *his* master, nor the servant above his lord. It is enough for the disciple that he be as his master, and the servant as his lord. If they have called the master of the house Beelzebub, *how much more shall they call them of his household?*" (Matt. 10:24–25, emphasis added).

I'd love to see *that* promise embroidered, framed, and hung in the office or home of every Christian leader in America. The Bible teaches us clearly: We are going to be hated and persecuted for doing what is right.

Face it, friend. If they called our perfect, precious Savior the prince of demons, they will do the same to us—or worse—and we have no right to demand anything better. Jesus never sinned. He never erred. And yet when He pursued acts of righteousness, kindness, healing, and justice, they hurled insults at Him, they hated Him, and they plotted His death.

The Lord said, "If the world hates you, you know that it has hated Me before it hated you. If you were of the world, the world would love its own; but because you are not of the world, but I chose you out of the world, therefore the world hates you. Remember the word that I said to you, 'A slave is not greater than his master.' If they persecuted Me, they will also persecute you; if they kept My word, they will keep yours also" (John 15:18-20).

Do They Hate You? Great Job!

Now, now, cheer up. In fact, rejoice! Jesus commands us to rejoice when our reputation is ruined on His account. "Blessed are you when men revile at you, and

persecute you, and say all kinds of evil against you falsely,
on account of Me. *Rejoice, and be glad,* for your reward in
heaven is great, for so they persecuted the prophets who
were before you" (Matt. 5:11-12, emphasis added). Luke
records it this way: "Blessed are you when men hate you,
and ostracize you, and heap insults upon you, and spurn
your name as evil, for the sake of the Son of Man. Be glad
in that day and leap *for joy,* for behold, your reward is
great in heaven; for in the same way their fathers used to
treat the prophets" (Luke 6:22-23, emphasis added).

Everyone Is Happy—What's Wrong?

If your reputation is perfectly intact on every front, if
you never irritate anyone, if you never make a stir, you
might be doing something wrong—or more likely, *you're
not doing something right.* "Woe to you when all men speak
well of you, for in the same way their fathers used to treat
the false prophets" (Luke 6:26). The Bible has a crystal
clear promise: "All who live godly in Christ Jesus shall
suffer persecution" (2 Tim. 3:12). If we never experience
persecution, if we never make a single soul angry (as
Christ often did), something is probably wrong. Probably
very wrong.

When we stand for the Lord Jesus and the laws of
God revealed in the Bible, it is inevitable that we will
offend someone. And in that hour we must not shrink
from our duty—no compromise. In that hour of trial the
unwholesome preservation of our reputation is of little or
no consequence to God. In fact, He might be trying to
smash the idol of reputation. The Prince of Life hung
naked and shamed on a cross for you and me in the
fulfillment of God's will. God has the right to require that
our reputation be laid in the dust in obedience to His will.
If we are mocked, falsely accused, berated, and maligned
for doing or saying what our Lord has commanded, so be
it. Blessed be His Name. He has given us the indescrib-
able privilege of experiencing the trials with the prophets
and of following in our Savior's blood-stained steps. As

the apostle Paul wrote, "For unto you it is given in behalf of Christ, not only to believe on him, but also to suffer for his sake" (Phil. 1:29).

"I'll Take a Padded Cross, Please"

The demand of discipleship for the Christian has never changed. It is simply this: death to self. We must pick up *our* cross daily (see Luke 9:23).

Consider this: We love the cross of Christ, and well we should. On that God-ordained cross our Savior was slain, our sins were atoned for, and we were redeemed to God. We embrace the cross of Christ, *but we despise and reject the cross He has commanded us to bear*—the believer's cross.

The believer's cross doesn't atone for our sins, it doesn't redeem us to God, and it doesn't make the sky grow dark. It simply kills us. Usually uneventful, un-historic, and unrecorded, the believer's cross is our call— nay, it is our *duty*—to lay our reputations, our self-pres-ervation, our very lives at the feet of the Lamb of God.

"For whether we live, we live unto the Lord; and whether we die, we die unto the Lord: whether we live therefore, or die, we are the Lord's" (Rom. 14:8). When we become the grain of wheat, falling into the ground and dying alone, then will we bear much fruit (John 12:24). You may desire to be used of God in a great way. Are you willing to go with Christ outside the establishment, or as the Bible puts it, "outside the city gate bearing His re-proach"? (Heb. 13:13). You may desire to speak for God before multitudes. Are you speaking for Him during your lunch hour at work? Are you declaring His Word to your relatives or neighbors? If you shrink back from speaking before the few for fear and love of your reputation, what makes you think you could withstand the blistering heat of prolonged public hatred?

Friend, if you have bowed the knee to the idol of reputation, repent. Ask God for forgiveness. And then ask Him for courage. As you meditate on these truths, certain situations, certain relationships, may come to your mind where you have not said or done what you should have. God will give you another chance. Each time He proves you, He will give you greater and greater responsibility and anointing for His kingdom. If you fail a test, don't despair. Again seek forgiveness—and prepare yourself for the make-up exam! There is no end to opportunities to die to ourselves, to stand for God in this troubling hour, and to lay our reputation at His nail-scarred feet.

May God help us to learn to loathe the preservation of our nice, safe, non-confrontational (uneventful, unfruitful) lives; may we learn to live out Christ's command that we hate our own lives in comparison to our love and zeal for Him (see John 12:25–26). When people are prepared to lay down their lives, they become very dangerous. Why? Because they are unafraid. They can't be bought off or cowed into silence. When we "love not our lives, even unto death" (Rev. 12:11), we will become truly dangerous to the enemies' armies and truly useful for the extension of our Master's kingdom.

So smash that idol of reputation!

Everyone here can save himself in his own fashion. To educate the young people into religious ways may perhaps be the task of the Church, but to educate the young in politics is very much our affair. . . . The youth belongs to us and we will yield them to no one. And the denominational press is equally superfluous. . . . For the Churches there is only one solution, which will ensure peace: Back into the sacristy. Let the Churches serve God; we serve the People.[1]

Josef Goebbels, 4 August 1935

Many of them (the clergy) were so deeply shocked by the tumultuous course of events in the first year of Nazi rule that their only wish was to withdraw from political involvement of any sort. Both their sense of loyalty to established power and their theological leanings, strongly influenced by the Pietistic tradition, inclined them towards a purely "spiritual" ministry, concerned only with individualistic salvation and ethics, and a readiness to obey the government's orders under all circumstances. On that account they were prepared to accept the Nazi dictum that "politics do not belong in the Church."[2]

Six

JUST PREACH
THE GOSPEL
(And Other Out of Balance Statements)

"I believe we need to share the gospel."

Just preach the gospel. Just preach the gospel. Just preach the gospel. Just preach . . . oh. I'm sorry. Was I droning? I must have slipped into the mantra of the average separatist Christian.

Babies are being murdered!

"Just preach the gospel," they tell us.

Neo-pagans are taking over! The White House and the Supreme Court have fallen under the control of God-haters!

"Just preach the gospel," they drone.

Planned Parenthood is brainwashing and corrupting children!

"Just preach the gospel," they insist.

Why? Why do they cling to an obviously inadequate solution?

Why Not Ask Why?

After years of observing this phenomenon and innumerable discussions and debates about this knee-jerk excuse for avoiding prophetic action, I have a good overview of "why."

As clearly as I can tell, the "preach the gospel" mindset falls into two distinct groups.

Group One views preaching the gospel as the social cure-all.

Group Two views society as incurable and terminally corrupt. They preach the gospel to snatch individuals out of this corrupt age, out of hell, and into heaven.

Let's explore both these views behind this worn-out cliché.

But before we do, let's step back and define our terms. What do I mean by "preach the gospel"? Or more importantly, what do "they" (that unnamed, unfaced group) mean by "preach the gospel"?

What "They" Mean by "Preach the Gospel"

After many years in the faith and innumerable conversations with Christians on this topic, this is what I understand us to be saying when we say we "preach the gospel" in its narrowest sense. God is Father, Son, and Holy Spirit. Christ the Son died for our sins so that we could be reconciled to God. He was buried, and on the third day He rose from the dead and ascended into heaven from whence He will return in power and glory to judge the living and the dead. He that believes in Him shall be saved; he that does not believe shall be damned. Many debate whether mere "faith" is enough, or whether repentance is also required. (Count me in the repentance group.) I realize this is a very cursory overview, not discussing redemption by blood, justification by faith, what compromises true faith, imputed righteousness, regeneration by the Holy Spirit and more, but for our purposes, I believe it will suffice and 99.9 percent would agree with this overview of the gospel (or at least know what I'm talking about).

One other critical observation: For both factions of the "just preach the gospel" crowd, it seems they believe it is either the believers' *sole* duty in this culture to "preach the gospel," or they think it is their "primary" duty. The primary duty of "preaching the gospel" is so paramount that it has the practical effect of being their sole activity, or at least their sole concern (or at least the sole benefi- ciary of their lip service). They believe our calling from God is to go from person to person, crowd to crowd preaching the gospel.

Medicine for Society

The "gospel as cure-all" crowd believes that as we keep preaching, society will become a better place be- cause of the influence of the gospel and because more and more individuals will be converting. The influence of the gospel and the salvation of certain individuals will result in better laws, more righteous television program- ming, more godly universities, better newspaper stories, etc.

Well, I hate to be the one to point out the emperor's naked rear-end, but something doesn't add up.

We have more "gospel preaching" in America than any other nation on earth. Yet America is growing more corrupt by the week; injustice in the courts is growing; oppression against Christians is on the rise; mockery of the holy has become common; homosexuals are demand- ing the right to be married and have children; television borders on the pornographic; pornography is growing more vile and violent; Nazi-like doctors want to kill the elderly and are harvesting aborted babies' body parts; our tax money pays for blasphemy. Need I go further?

All of our gospel preaching hasn't stopped a tidal wave of iniquity from sweeping over America, a tidal wave that threatens our very survival.

Furthermore, we've probably had more people say "the sinner's prayer" who claim to be "born again" than in any other nation on earth. We have more churches, more gospel radio, gospel television, gospel literature, gospel tracts, street meetings, evangelistic crusades, gos- pel music, "win the world, win your town, and win your neighbor to the Lord" training seminars than any nation on earth. American Christians spend more money on domestic and foreign missions than any other group of people on the planet. And yet, America is fast becoming the moral cesspool of the earth.

If the "just preach the gospel" solution was an agenda for cultural reformation, we should see the millennium practically in progress! But obviously something is drastically wrong with this simplistic, detached solution— and it's time we accept that fact. The "just preach the gospel" game plan for victory is a categoric, colossal failure.

In all fairness, this "social solution" seems reasonable, and in a way it is. If everyone at CBS, from Dan Rather to the entertainment division, became Christians tomorrow, we would expect a difference in the way the news is reported and what types of movies are shown. (Unless they were "discipled" in Jesse Jackson's church.)

However, the real problem with this battle plan is that it severely limits the scope of the church's role in the earth. In fact, I would say it has had a crippling effect on the ability of the church to be salt and light in this nation.

The same Bible that commands us to "go into all the world" commands us to rebuke the ruthless, to defend the fatherless, to care for the widow, to speak up for the oppressed (see Psalm 82:1-4; Proverbs 24:10-12, 31:8-9). In fact, *true religion* before God is to help the widow and orphan in their distress (James 1:27). If we fail in our biblically commanded societal duties, our very worship becomes a stench in God's nostrils, and He has promised *not* to hear our prayers (see Isaiah 1:10-18). He said in verse 15, "And when ye spread forth your hands, I will hide mine eyes from you; yea, when ye make many prayers, I will not hear: your hands are full of blood."

Not Either-Or

The cure of America's illness is not an either/or proposition. Preaching the gospel is not in conflict with social reformation and visa versa. Both are critical. God's concern is for the spirit, soul, and body. Our goal should be the whole counsel of God. God's Word explains how fallen men can be reconciled to God. God's Word instructs the individual, the family, the church, and the state in how they can please God. God's Word provides clear direction for all of life's affairs, and as Christians we are to herald the entirety of God's Word.

Do God a Service—Put a Pornographer in Jail

For example: A pornographer needs to be converted to Christ. We should call him to repentance and share our faith in Christ with him. At the same time, we should be confronting and exposing his business and trying to get him put in jail for his criminal behavior. If the laws against pornography in his community aren't being enforced, we should be working to replace the sheriff or the district attorney with a God-fearing leader who will uphold the law and punish the guilty.

"But why not just preach the gospel, and forget about these 'worldly' tactics?"

What you call a "worldly tactic" is actually a godly, God-ordained duty to rebuke and punish the wicked.

Furthermore, God is deeply concerned for the young men and women whose minds will be warped permanently by exposure to filth; God is deeply grieved for the young girls and boys who will be molested and forever marred by men who are slaves to the demon of pornography, men who use pornography to disarm and molest children. (One police study showed pornography was involved in 80 percent of child molestation cases.) And as anyone who has dealt with victims of sexual abuse can tell you, simply hearing and believing the gospel does not instantaneously heal someone nor set them free from the pain, the false guilt, the anguish, or the horrifying memories of sexual abuse.

Our churches are filled with women who have been sexually abused. Yes, they are on their way to heaven, but in the meantime their lives are riddled or even filled with pain. Other women—who never make it into our churches—become hostages of the pornographic under-world, slaves in prostitution, or simply wind up in successive abusive relationships.

In that light, you can see how it is in everyone's best spiritual interest for the church to demand that law enforcement hammer pornographers. We must expend energy in both "preaching the gospel" in the narrow sense, as well as "living the gospel"—the good news that the Lord is come—and extending the rule of His authority into all arenas.

Let's face it, the "just preach the gospel" as a cure-all for social ills isn't working. In fact, it could be labeled a colossal failure. We must keep preaching the gospel, but we must also herald the whole Word of God and extend the authority of God into every citadel of power.

Another Notch on My Evangelistic Belt

For Group Two—the snatch 'em from hell crowd—I have much less patience and even a little contempt. Let me explain.

This "gospel only" crowd is prepared to tolerate every injustice, ignore every oppression, as long as they can share "The Four Spiritual Laws" with everybody. The world is going to hell and is irretrievable. It will get worse and worse, and there is nothing we can do to stop it. To be involved in politics, the care of the poor, the care of the elderly, is to preach a "social gospel." And heaven knows, we are *not* called to preach "social gospel." We're just supposed to get souls into heaven.

Let me give a couple of examples how this plays out.

Jesus—The Hard-Hearted Savior

I have had people tell me that they are not involved in pro-life because Jesus has called them to preach the gospel.

Translation: Jesus would have us stand idly by while a murderer ripped the arms and legs off a little girl and then crushed her head. We should do nothing to intervene, because Christ hasn't called us to. But He does want us to give a gospel tract to the murderer and smile and say, "Jesus loves you."

Moreover, *Jesus Himself* would not get involved. I had a man write and tell me that in Jesus' day, infanticide was a regular practice, and Christ did nothing to stop it. In other words, Jesus of Nazareth would walk by a crying baby girl left outside to be eaten by animals so that He could be about the Father's business—winning souls. This is a blasphemous portrayal of Christ.

"In fact," they say, "all those babies who are being aborted are better off—they're going directly to heaven!" (I've had Christians tell me this.) It saves the soul-winners a lot of work.

Others say, "We shouldn't fight against pornography. It's just a symptom. The real problem is sin. Just preach the gospel!"

Translation: While God-hating pagans traffic in the bodies and souls of women, children, and men, and while the porno shops sell filth that ends up corrupting and destroying youth—including church youth—you don't have to get into a long, distasteful, confrontational battle to close the porno shop. You don't have to confront the owners of convenience stores that sell women's bodies like lunch meat over the counter, nor do you have to boycott these stores and inconvenience yourself—just give a gospel tract and say, "God loves you."

These misguided Christians have separated most of the Bible and its mandates from life and law. For them the Bible is a handbook on personal salvation and personal holiness and happiness, but little more. This gives them a warped, unbiblical view of life and Christian duty.

If They Are "Gospel Preachers," I the More!

At this point I would like to speak as Paul spoke to the Corinthians and discuss a part of my persona—one that is seldom seen in front of the camera: the evangelist.

I am a gospel preacher. For example, ever since I became a Christian, I have picked up hitchhikers and told them of God's grace and mercy extended to us through the death of Christ. When I have a sinner in the car, I don't focus on the moral collapse of Western civilization, I focus on their need for Christ.

As my wife and friends will testify, many are the times I have shared Christ with store clerks, food servers, and cab drivers; many are the times I have preached in airports or in the street, both in America and in Central American countries. One time I exited a radio studio in downtown Pittsburgh after being a guest on a big radio show around midnight. I was shocked to see a group of listless teen-agers hanging around at a bus stop. To the surprise of my hosts, I walked up to them, put down my briefcase, and preached Christ to them. They listened, then we left.

Finally, because of the doors God has opened for me, I have the opportunity to preach Christ to many who may not hear it often—folks like Fay Wattleton, Patricia Ireland, Kate Michelman, Phil Donahue, Senator Bob Packwood—just to name a few. Many are the times I have preached Christ to college students, high-school students, and especially to angry mobs of pro-abortion activists. We recently led to the Lord a pro-abortion activist who had tailed us for three years. When we saw her at an event, we took the time to share Christ with her. She has left her pro-abortion activism and is regularly attending a Spirit-filled church.

I give this background for two reasons:

1. To show that I believe in preaching the gospel. When I take rhetorical shots at the "I'm *just* called to preach the gospel" mindset, I am *not* taking shots at preaching the gospel, but rather I am challenging a deficient, out-of-balance view of what our duty as Christians is to this generation. Offering salvation is critical, but our duties do not end there.

2. I preach the gospel to the lost regularly. Many

Christians who duck taking action under the excuse of "We're called to preach the gospel" seldom actually preach the gospel to the lost. For many, it may have become an excuse to vindicate their laziness or cowardice.

I have to wonder how many ministers who use this line are able to preach to sinners regularly, and how many just preach in their pulpits, week after week, to the same old crew. Being salt and light in the great cultural battlefields of our day puts us in direct contact with myriads of sinners. Activists who preach the gospel probably preach to more sinners in one day of demonstrating than a pastor who seldom preaches outside his pulpit does in the course of a year.

We're living what they're preaching.

God help us to live and preach the whole counsel of God. God help us to see that if we're being taxed to death, the cure might not be sharing "The Four Spiritual Laws." The cure might be to work feverishly to eject the socialist, messianic statists from office and replace them with God-fearing statesmen.

As the Bible says, "When the righteous are in authority, the people rejoice: but when the wicked beareth rule, the people mourn" (Prov. 29:2). Where would you rather live—in freedom or oppression? Who would you rather have rule, the righteous or the wicked? Where would you rather "preach the gospel"—in America, where you can still preach with much liberty, or in China, where you'll probably spend years in jail for preaching? Even gospel preaching fares better in a society where Christians are active in every realm of society, culture, and law.

Maybe we need to look at Christ's words a little more closely: "All authority is given unto me in heaven *and in earth.* Go ye therefore, and teach all nations, baptizing them in the name of the Father, and of the Son, and of the Holy Ghost: teaching them to observe all things whatsoever I have commanded you: and, lo, I am with you always, even unto the end of the world" (Matt. 28:18-20, emphasis added).

Neither in earlier times nor today has the Party the intention of waging any kind of war against Christianity. The Nazi State will however not tolerate under any circumstances any new or any continued political activity of the denominations. Let there be no misunderstanding about the resolve of the Party and the State on this matter! We attacked the political clergy once and got rid of them from the parliaments at a time when we had no power behind us and the other side had it all. But today we have the power and can defend these principles better. We will not conduct this struggle as one directed against Christianity or against only one of the two denominations. But we will ensure the purging from our public life of all those priests who have mistaken their profession and who ought to have been politicians and not pastors.[1]

Adolf Hitler

With the refusal of most Churchmen to follow a course of political and theological "disloyalty", hopes for a centre of resistance to Nazism quickly faded, while Luther's supposed teaching of obedience to the state was extended and misinterpreted to cover the submission of increasing numbers of Churchmen.[2]

Seven

THE BATTLE OF ALLEGIANCES

(The Good Guys vs. The Bad Guys)

*"After many years in Christian ministry, I don't believe
the Lord wants us to use force. . . . They aren't Christians you
know—they don't believe it's a life."*

Ultimately, the battle we are engaged in is a battle of
allegiances. Remember that. In fact, you may want to
quote it out loud:

"THE BATTLE FOR AMERICA'S SOUL IS A BATTLE
OF ALLEGIANCES."

There are only two sides. Those who hold their ethical allegiance to the Ten Commandments and those who
don't.

The question is: Whose god, and whose god's law,
will dominate this culture? Will it be the Triune God of
the Bible and His Law and principles? Or will it be man—
secular humanism—and the current whim of man?

I know this "black and white" view of the world
troubles a lot of people. But I see very little "grey" in the
Bible. Jesus said it clearly: "He that is not for Me is against
Me" (Matt. 12:30).

If we do not self-consciously make God's Law the
foundation of our culture, then we have no concrete foundation upon which to build; we have no unchanging moral

code upon which to base our laws. In fact, we lose the ability to define right and wrong. The very concepts of "right" and "wrong," "good" and "evil," are intrinsically biblical.

Moreover, without an unchanging moral code on which to build society, we lose the very ability to govern. Moral anarchy produces social and legal anarchy.

For those who believe these are the words of a religious fanatic, let me quote another religious zealot, George Washington:

> Of all the dispositions and habits which lead to political prosperity, *religion* and *morality* are indispensable supports. In vain would that man claim the tribute of patriotism who should labor to subvert these great pillars of human happiness—these firmest props of the duties of men and citizens. The mere politician, equally with the pious man, ought to respect and to cherish them. A volume could not trace all their connections with private and public felicity. Let it simply be asked, Where is the security for property, for reputation, for life, if the sense of religious obligation *desert* the oaths which are the instruments of investigation in courts of justice? And let us with caution indulge the supposition that morality can be maintained without religion. Whatever may be conceded to the influence of refined education on minds of peculiar structure, *reason and experience both forbid us to expect that national morality can prevail in exclusion of religious principle.*[3] (from Farewell Address, 17 September 1796, emphasis added)

First Principles

Allow me to state my presupposition: All human law to be legitimate must be rooted in biblical principles, and all biblical principles are rooted in the Ten Commandments. Hence, the Ten Commandments must be the foundation of our society. Without the Ten Commandments to define right and wrong, we are in a moral free fall.

But our enemies—and some deceived or gullible Christians—will yell, "But this is a pluralistic society! You must have separation of church and state!" We agree on that, but we cannot tolerate the separation of the state and state officials from biblical ethics. Otherwise we'll have a bunch of atheistic, idolatrous, blaspheming, rebellious, lying, thieving, adulterating, covetous neo-pagans running the country, passing laws that reflect their greed and avarice. (It kinda has a Ted Kennedy-Barney Frank-Bob Packwood feel to it.) *That* is why we need social/political reformation along biblical guidelines.

You CAN Legislate Morality!

I can hear our enemies whine their familiar argument: "You cannot impose your morality on us! You cannot legislate morality!"

Oh really?

This argument has worked brilliantly, but if you think about it, it is probably close to the most asinine reasoning you've ever heard (and we who believe it are either ignorant or gullible or deceived). Why? Why is the statement, "You can't legislate morality," idiotic? *Because all law is the imposition of morality.*

Laws against theft are the result of non-thieves imposing their morality on would-be thieves. Laws against rape are the result of non-rapists imposing their morality on would-be rapists. In fact, even laws against speeding are the imposition of a majority of lawmakers' morality about speeding on the rest of us. *All* law is the imposition of morality.

Can you imagine the folly of a thief standing up and saying, "I demand freedom of choice! Freedom of conscience! You non-thieves have imposed your morals on me! This violates the separation of church and state!"

I will say it again for emphasis' sake: Arguments against "imposing our morals" and "legislating morality" are moronic—but the propaganda has worked marvelously. God help us.

Whose Morality Will Prevail?

The question is not whether morals will be imposed, but *whose* morals will be imposed. The question is not *can* we legislate morality, but rather *whose morality will be legislated.*

Will God's Law or paganism be the foundation for the morals that are imposed? Will God's Law or humanism (i.e., man is the center of the universe and can determine his own morality) be the source of the morality that is legislated? Those are the only two choices. Either we base our laws on the unchanging, perfect Law of God, or we build on the shifting sand of the whims of man.

For example, take the humanistic view of homosexual behavior. In the 1940s it was considered a perverse, criminal behavior. In the 1950s it was considered an illness. In the 1960s, "Hey dude, it's pretty weird, but if that's what you're into . . ." In the 1970s, homosexuals "came out of the closet" and wanted tolerance. In the 1980s, sodomites wanted special minority rights under the law. In the 1990s, sodomites want the right to be "married," they want to recruit and indoctrinate our children into their perversion (via public schools), and they want to banish all dissent against their vile lifestyle by instituting "hate crime" laws. They call us "homophobes."

In contrast, the Bible's view of homosexual behavior has not changed. Sodomy is an abomination. It is criminal behavior.

Hell's Party Line

Yet, in spite of glaring examples such as this, many Christians have either implicitly or explicitly believed the lie that we cannot "legislate morality." It's time to slap ourselves in the face and wake up! When a Christian foolishly declares that we can't legislate morals, he is parroting hell's party line.

Let me say it like this: The Ten Commandments—the Law God gave Moses and confirmed and fulfilled in the

Lord Jesus Christ—must be the foundation for our nation's laws and cultural norms. We must self-consciously seek to build our families, churches, government, educational institutions, hospitals, businesses—*everything*—on the Laws and principles of the Word of God.

Our Goal? A Christian Nation

Let me say it clearly: We want a Christian nation. I know this will make the heathen howl—and a good number of pluralist evangelists too. But the only alternative is a pagan nation. By "Christian nation," I don't mean that everyone is forced to be a Christian or forced to go to church or to believe in God. People are free to be Buddhists or atheists. What I mean by a Christian nation is a nation whose laws are self-consciously built on the laws and principles of the Bible. For those who feel this is too radical, let me quote a couple of radical Supreme Court decisions:

Church of The Holy Trinity vs. United States
Supreme Court 1892—"Our laws and our institutions must necessarily be based upon and embody the teaching of the Redeemer of mankind. It is impossible that it should be otherwise, and in this sense and to this extent our civilization and our institutions are emphatically Christian." (In this case, eighty-seven precedents were given for the decision.)

Vidal vs. Girards
Supreme Court 1844—This case had to do with a school in Philadelphia that wanted to teach morality without using the Bible. The court ruled that it could not do so, saying:
"The purest principles of morality are to be taught [in schools]. Where are they found? Whoever searches for them must go to the source from which a Christian man derives his faith—the Bible."

The Presidents Speak

Former presidents—who were not concerned about being chic or politically correct—made bold declarations concerning the place of the Bible in our law and culture. If these men were in office today, the ACLU might call for their crucifixion, and the godless press would lead the charge! Consider their words:

George Washington: "It is impossible to rightly govern the world without God and the Bible."[4]

Woodrow Wilson: "The Bible . . . is the one supreme source of revelation of the meaning of life, the nature of God and spiritual nature and need of men. It is the only guide of life which really leads the spirit in the way of peace and salvation. America was born a Christian nation. America was born to exemplify that devotion to the elements of righteousness which are derived from the revelations of Holy Scripture." He also said: "There are a good many problems before the American people today, and before me as President, but I expect to find the solution to those problems just in the proportion that I am faithful in the study of the Word of God."[5]

Calvin Coolidge: "The foundations of our society and our government rest so much on the teachings of the Bible that it would be difficult to support them if faith in these teachings would cease to be practically universal in our country."[6]

Harry Truman: "The fundamental basis of this nation's law was given to Moses on the Mount. The fundamental basis of our Bill of Rights comes from the teachings we get from Exodus and St. Matthew, from Isaiah and St. Paul. I don't think we emphasize that enough these days. If we don't have the proper fundamental moral background, we will finally wind up with a totalitarian government which does not believe in rights for anybody but the state."[7]

For those yet unconvinced, let me ask you some questions. If we don't use the Bible as our framework for right and wrong then what are we left with? The latest CBS-*New York Times* poll?

The will of the majority? Majority rule could be hell on earth. For example, what if a vast majority of Americans want to own non-whites as slaves? What if a vast majority of Americans want to gas Jews in concentration camps? If unrestrained "democracy" is the ultimate goal, then the majority would be "right." On what basis could we resist them? *Only the unchanging Word of God.*

Confusion in the Camp

Tragically, many Christian leaders have told Christian activists not to mention God, the Bible, or the Ten Commandments in our public debate on the issues. They encourage us rather to talk about "traditional family values."

Unfortunately, many Christians have followed their advice and have taken up the language of the "moderates." Rather than speak in the name of God, they speak in the generic, fluctuating name of "conservatism" and "traditional family values."

The question is, *whose* tradition? The feminists? The homosexuals? The phrase "traditional family values" has become void of meaning. For example, a billboard recently was erected in the Los Angeles area picturing two lesbians with the words, "Another Traditional Family."

I offer another example. I was recently in a radio studio in a major city where the co-chair of the Mayor's Committee on Homosexual Rights was being interviewed. The reporter asked her, "Does anyone on the Mayor's Commission hold to traditional family values?"

"Oh, yes," she assured him. "Many on the Commission hold to traditional values."

The reporter pressed the point. "Does anyone on the Commission believe homosexuality is sin?"

She got angry. "Well, that's quite a leap from believing in traditional family values to believing homosexuality is a sin!"

Get my point? For her, Adam and Steve were as good a "tradition" as Adam and Eve.

Frankly, I'm tired of hearing about "traditional family values." We believe in *biblical* family values.

Stealth Christians

One of the huge errors of the "Christian Right" since the late 1970s in America is that we refused to identify ourselves and our policies in the political arena as *distinctly Christian*. We preferred instead to be called "conservatives." Well, what do we base our beliefs on? The Bible? Then say so, without embarrassment. Heaven and earth will pass away—but God's Word will never pass away.

If we duck and dodge, bob and weave, and refuse to say, "Thus says the Word of God" in the political arena, it's our feelings against theirs. It's our ideas against theirs. They are "liberal" Humanists and we have become "conservative" Humanists. We both hang our beliefs on what we prefer—or on the latest slickly worded poll.

And remember this: the conservative Humanist will usually cave in to or compromise with the demands and morality of the liberal Humanist. For example, I was just watching Phil Donahue debate a "conservative" on CNBC about "homophobia" and America's supposed need to indoctrinate children to "tolerate" and accept the sodomite lifestyle. The "liberal" wanted to do it in first grade. What was the "conservative" response? "No, teach them in the sixth grade."

What conviction! What a pillar of strength! He had already surrendered to the indoctrination demands of the godless. He was simply grasping for the least repulsive terms of surrender, so he could call his defeat "moderation."

The Christian position is clear: Homosexuality is an abomination, and we do not teach "tolerance" of a perverse criminal behavior, any more than we would teach "tolerance" of pedophilia or rape (or cocaine dealing or embezzlement).

God help us to see what is at stake! Either America will be rebuilt on the Laws and principles in the Word of God, *or she will perish*. The Word of God is the rock upon which families, churches, nations (and all institutions in them) must be built. All else is shifting sand. And as Jesus warned—all houses built on sand will collapse. And their fall—our fall—will be an unspeakable calamity.

If you think my words are those of a religious zealot, a right-wing fundamentalist nut, let me introduce you to one of my heroes: Theodore Roosevelt. Consider Roosevelt's warnings:

> Progress has brought us both unbounded opportunities and unbridled difficulties. Thus, the measure of our civilization will not be *that* we have done much, but *what* we have done with that much. I believe that the next half century will determine if we will advance the cause of Christian civilization or revert to the horrors of brutal paganism. The thought of modern industry in the hands of Christian charity is a dream worth dreaming. The thought of industry in the hands of paganism is a nightmare beyond imagining. The choice between the two is upon us.[8]

Roosevelt cut to the heart of this war of allegiances.

> There are those who believe that a new modernity demands a new morality. What they fail to consider is the harsh reality that there is no such thing as a new morality. There is only one morality. All else is immorality. There is only true Christian ethics over against which stands the whole of paganism. If we are to fulfill our great destiny as a people, then we must return to the old morality, the sole morality.[9]

Would to God our forefathers had heeded his warning.

Or consider the words of John Adams in 1798. America was on the brink of an unwanted war with France, a war we could have easily lost.

John Adams understood the direct connection between a nation's obedience to God and its ability to survive as a free nation. He understood that threatening calamities

were the judgment of God, and he called on people to
pray and repent.

From "A Proclamation by the President of the United
States of America":

> As the safety and prosperity of nations ultimately
> and essentially depend on the protection and the bless-
> ing of Almighty God, and the national acknowledge-
> ment of this truth is not only an indispensable duty
> which the people owe to Him, but a duty whose
> natural influence is favorable to the promotion of that
> morality and piety without which social happiness
> can not exist nor the blessings of a free government
> be enjoyed; and as this duty, at all times incumbent,
> is so especially in seasons of difficulty or of danger,
> when existing or threatening calamities, the just judg-
> ments of God against prevalent iniquity, are a loud
> call to repentance and reformation . . .

> I have therefore thought fit to recommend, and I do
> hereby recommend, that Wednesday, the 9th day of
> May next, be observed throughout the United States
> as a day of solemn humiliation, fasting, and prayer;
> that the citizens of these States, abstaining on that
> day from their customary worldly occupations, offer
> their devout addresses to the Father of Mercies agree-
> ably to those forms or methods which they have sev-
> erally adopted as the most suitable and becoming;
> that all religious congregations do, with the deepest
> humility, acknowledge before God the manifold sins
> and transgressions with which we are justly charge-
> able as individuals and as a nation, beseeching Him
> at the same time, of His infinite grace, through the
> Redeemer of the World, freely to remit all our of-
> fenses, and to incline us by His Holy Spirit to that
> sincere repentance and reformation which may af-
> ford us reason to hope for his inestimable favor and
> heavenly benediction.[10]

We too are at war—a cultural civil war, a war of
allegiances. If righteousness is going to prevail, if paganism is going to be turned back, then we must move to
restore this nation to being a Christian nation. Otherwise

we will lose the war for America's soul, and the United States as we know it will perish.

And if we are going to reform and rebuild our country, we're going to have to deliberately infiltrate the power bases of America. We'll deliberately have to raise up men like John Adams and Teddy Roosevelt to be "morally correct," not "politically correct" statesmen. May God grant it.

There is but one German people, and there can therefore be but one German youth. And there can be but one German Youth Movement, because there is but one way in which German youth can be educated and trained. The handful of people, who perhaps still cherish within themselves the thought that, beginning with the youth, they will be able to divide the German nation again, will be disappointed. This Reich stands, and is building itself up anew, upon its youth. And this Reich will hand over its youth to no one, but will take its education and its formation upon itself.[1]

Adolf Hitler, 1 May 1937

Eight

CULTURALLY ILLITERATE, SOCIALLY IRRELEVANT

(Lamebrains Are Us)

*"You can't expect those pro-chance people—what do you call them—pro-*chance?"

I still love watching Bugs Bunny and Elmer Fudd. (All right, so the kid in me is still alive. What can I say?) Bugs Bunny gets him spinning in circles, with Elmer pathetically repeating his confession of confusion, "Which way did he go? Which way did he go?"

Welcome to the world of Christian Elmer Fudds. We're confused. Out of touch. Ignorant. Spinning in circles. And perhaps above all else, gullible.

Why? Because we are ignorant. When we are ignorant, we are gullible. We become prey. We American Christians tend to be ignorant concerning vast sections of our culture such as our educational institutions, our government, big business, foreign affairs, foreign policy, how the media works, how the media and press deceive us, and on and on.

When that dear man said "pro-chance" I could have laughed. I also could have cried. Here is a Christian who cares enough for humanity that he is evangelizing in jail, and yet he is ignorant of the name of the "bad guys" in the greatest moral conflict in our nation's history, ignorant of one of the most hideous, unspeakable holocausts in world history. Is it any wonder we are losing this nation's soul?

The Elmer Fudd syndrome is not just in the pro-life battle. Our ignorance and social irrelevance permeates every sphere of life, with the possible exception of church and family. And at times I question how much we understand these.

For example, let me give you a little quiz in the area of government.

The Federal Government

How many U.S. senators does America have?

How long are their terms?

How many members are in the House of Representatives?

How long are their terms?

What are the names of your senators and congressmen? (Oooh)

How many U.S. Supreme Court judges are there?

How do they get on the bench? (What is the "bench"?)

How long is their term of office?

How is the U.S. Constitution amended (or changed)?

I know, those were easy. Let me ask you some more difficult questions—but the answers to these are perhaps more critical to us.

State and Local Government

How many members are in your state senate and assembly?

How do your local, county, and state judges get in office? Are they elected or appointed?

If appointed, by whom?

How long is their term?

What kind of city, town, or county government do you have?

How does a law become a law in your state?

In your town?

In your nation?

Who is your district attorney?

Is your district attorney (or state attorney or prosecutor) elected or appointed?

If appointed, by whom?

For how long?

Political Nitty Gritty

Here's where it gets really hard—but really important.

What is a precinct?

What is a committeeman?

How does someone become a committeeman?

If you are registered in a party (Democrat, Republican, or other) who decides what your party's state platform is? Who decides the national platform?

Do you know what a party platform is?

How does a candidate for office get a party's endorsement?

How does someone run for office, i.e., how do they get on the ballot for school board, or for state assemblyman?

How does someone run *from* office? (Oops, only kidding.)

The World

Let's talk about foreign affairs.

How does the U.S. make a treaty with another nation, whether friend or foe?

Who elects or appoints our ambassadors?

Who does the Constitution say has the power to declare war?

Who is in charge of our armed services?

(As I was writing this in jail, I was interrupted by a policeman from another force. He made a special trip over here to shake my hand, and tell me he is a Christian, and that he agrees with what I'm doing. Talk about irony—God help us.)

I've asked you very basic questions about one area of American life—our government. Many more similar questions could be posed.

Now I have a little object lesson for you.

Three Spheres Minus One = Oppression

The next time you go to your local Christian bookstore, take a look around. Ask the clerk to point you to the section on family (and healing dysfunctional families). Then ask him to show you the section on churches and church growth (and healing dysfunctional churches). Then ask for the section on government. (There are no books on healing dysfunctional politicians—*yet*.) You'll probably get a perplexed look because there probably isn't a government section. You'll get sent to that eclectic section, "issues."

We are inundated with tapes, books, videos, teachings, and pamphlets on the church and the family, but we have studiously ignored the one institution that can wreak havoc on our churches and families—*the government*. This is suicidal.

I know you've gone to prayer meetings. I know you've gone to seminars on marriage and family. When was the last time you attended a meeting on how to remove and replace a godless judge? Or how to confront and replace a district attorney who won't prosecute pornographers but comes down hard on pro-lifers? What seminar did you attend teaching you how to take back your school board and/or throw out Planned Parenthood or some godless "sex ed" curriculum from your school?

I know you've sacrificed for a church fund raiser—whether through a pledge or a bake sale. But have you ever sacrificed to get a Christian in some political office?

Have you ever gone door to door collecting signatures for a righteous candidate, or handing out literature for his election?

And again, we are only talking about infiltrating government!

The Power Bases Need You!

What about education? Medicine? Journalism?

How does "social services" work? What currently constitutes child abuse in your state? You may be guilty of "child abuse" if you discipline your children according to biblical standards—and some low-level bureaucrat thug (or slug) who is hostile to Christians could make your life miserable. The numbers of godly Christian parents who are being accused of "child abuse" are growing constantly. How did we get in this mess?

When is the last time you had an altar call in your church for political activists? We take our brightest and our best youth and say to them, "Become a preacher! Become a missionary!" Why not say, "Become a principal!" or "Become a dean of a university!" or "Become a judge!" or a lawyer, or a governor, or a mayor, or a councilman, or an educator, or a doctor, or an artist, or a journalist, or a president.

Total Collapse Calls for Comprehensive Rebuilding

America's moral collapse is comprehensive. Our strategy to rebuild the waste places on the bedrock of biblical principles must also be comprehensive. This means we have to know what we're doing and what we're saying.

"Oh, Brother Randy, this is too overwhelming! I'm a mom trying to raise kids!" Or, "I'm a dad trying to earn a living!" Or, "I'm a student trying to finish school!" Well, I'm not trying to overwhelm you; I'm trying to give you a big picture vision.

First of all, read. Turn your television off. Obviously you *can* read, because you're reading this. Read books on how to reform our culture with biblical principles. Don't read too many books on being wealthy, or Christian novels, or how to lower your cholesterol. Obviously those books aren't necessarily wrong, but our nation is dying. When a patient is dying, you don't give them a haircut or a manicure. You pour all your energy into saving the patient. You've only got so much time—so you need to spend it reading books that will help us through the crisis.

We also need to know our roots and to see whence we've fallen, so you must read books on history. Knowing history is critical to leading in the future. (I've given you a small list in the back.) Get audio cassettes and videos that address the same needs.

We all have time somewhere to read, watch, or listen. In the car, when the kids are asleep, on our lunch hour—we have time somewhere. The issue isn't time, it's *vision*. Once you catch the vision to bring this culture back to a biblical foundation, you will discipline yourself and do what it takes to become an active duty soldier of righteousness.

Or to put it this way, if you were a Jew in ancient Israel with a vision to fight the Philistines, you would do it by whatever means available: a sword, a spear, a sling and a stone, or the jawbone of an ass. Vision precedes strategy. Vision develops strategy. Vision drives strategy. Vision is willing to alter strategy.

And so I challenge you: Pray to God for a vision to recapture the power bases of our culture. Read your Bible for vision and strategy. And read books that deal with the crisis at hand. Then we will be fit for the task.

In the long run the Church question is a question of the young people. This is not only a matter of their education through the Hitler Youth but also by their parents. The less the parents' opposition is aroused on Church matters, the less they will inculcate in their children's opposition to the teachings of the Hitler Youth.[1]

Rudolf Hess

The creation of an ideologically objective school system is one of the most important tasks of the Party and the State. In order to achieve this goal, the remains of denominational [Christian] influence must be completely removed from our German education system wherever it still appears.[2]

Martin Bormann

My pedagogy is strict. Every weakness must be hammered out. In my new training schools, young people will grow who will shock the world. I want a powerful, masterly, cruel and fearless youth. . . . They must be able to bear pain. There must be nothing weak or tender about them. The freedom and dignity of the wild beast must shine from their eyes. . . . That is how I will root out a thousand years of human domestication. Then I will have the pure noble material in front of me; and then I can make something new.[3]

Adolf Hitler

Nine

THE MAGIC WAND
(Or How You Can Be Lazy, Dumb, and Fat and Just Pray Away the Results)

"I don't believe God would have us use force to change their minds. He just wants us to pray."

I'll never forget the event. Five thousand or more Christians had gathered in Washington, D.C., at the Washington Monument to raise their voices against child-killing. The backstage area was filled with Christian leaders. Speaker after speaker boldly declared their steadfast stand on behalf of innocent children and needy mothers.

And then, with an aura of dynamic spiritual authority, a Christian leader took the microphone and said, "Now, stand to your feet, brothers and sisters. We are going to bind the spirit of abortion over this city."

He had everybody bow their heads and stretch out their hands while he boomed forth in demanding tones, "Satan! We come against you . . ."

While he was praying and rebuking, my heart was grieving. Why? Because I knew that at that moment babies were dying all over D.C. and that his prayer wasn't preventing their death. Moreover, I thought, "Oh, God, if these five thousand people would just 'put some feet on their prayers,' and bodily go down to the killing centers, we would save many babies." But it was not to be.

I call it "The Spiritual Magic Wand." You can confess it, rebuke it, speak it, claim it, agree on it, and poof!—it's going to happen. (Yeah, sure. Tell me another one.) The shipwrecked faith of thousands whose wand didn't work testifies to the dangerous imbalance of these doctrines. We've been led to believe that all problems—small and large, personal and national, physical and emotional—can be dealt with in prayer.

Obviously, prayer is critical (as I will discuss in a moment), but prayer is often not enough. We must act when we can act, taking bold steps of obedience to God.

Action Equals Love

For those who think I'm putting too much emphasis on what we do, as opposed to what we pray, consider the story of the Good Samaritan (Luke 10:25-37). Perhaps the priest prayed when he passed by, "Oh Lord, save this poor man!" Perhaps the Levite bound the devil. "I rebuke the spirit of ditch beating over this man!" But neither one helped the man. Neither one loved his neighbor. And neither one pleased God.

Consider the judgment of the sheep and goats (Matt. 25:31-46). *Prayer isn't even mentioned.* Christ's judgment was based solely on what men did or didn't do on behalf of His brethren. "Depart from me, ye cursed, into everlasting fire, prepared for the devil and his angels. . . . Inasmuch as ye did *it* not to one of the least of these, ye did *it* not to me" (verses 41 and 45).

Action Birthed by Prayer

Now please, don't misunderstand me. When God "called" me to fight against child-killing—or should I say the moment I became aware of God's call on my life, I was in a prayer meeting. It was October of 1983. We were praying for God to bring an end to abortion. In that time of prayer, God put His finger on me and drafted me into the war to end child-killing. And He made it very clear to me that I was to physically strive for children's lives, not just pray.

Herein lies the balance: Prayer and action. Prayer *and* action.

After I was active 2 1/2 years in pro-life work, Operation Rescue was born in my heart in March of 1986. That too was during a time of prayer and meditation on the Scriptures. Operation Rescue was born in prayer, and has been sustained by prayer.

Anyone who has ever been to our Operation Rescue rallies or a rescue knows that in many ways it's a large prayer meeting. We break up into groups, and plead with God to help us end child-killing. We beseech Him to have mercy on our nation. Clergy lead in prayers of repentance. We jointly read and pray the prayers of the Scriptures.

I believe God wants us to pray. I have seen the hand of God move again and again in a multitude of situations, in what was undoubtedly an answer to our prayers.

Furthermore, now more than ever the church needs desperately to pray prayers of deep repentance and mourning. Psalm 51 should be prayed with tears in our eyes, with a broken and contrite heart. We need to be like Daniel, identifying with the sins of the people of God, beseeching God for His mercy in this hour.

Moreover, we should pray that God would confuse His enemies' camp, that He would thwart His enemies' plans—both human and demonic; that as He did for Jehoshaphat, He would cause the enemies to turn on each other.

My objective is not to belittle prayer. God forbid. My objective is to expose the folly of our current wishful thinking about prayer. My goal is for Christians to stop using praying as a justification for laziness or cowardice.

You've heard: "We'll just commit it to the Lord and see what He does" (while we sit and watch television).

"You know, you can't make things better in politics, you've just got to pray about it." (We aren't even registered to vote.)

"The battle is the Lord's. He doesn't want us to use

the arm of the flesh—we've got to pray and leave the results to Him." (Any strategies to close an abortion mill or porno shop that include *hard work* are the arm of the flesh.)

Now, I understand that many situations exist that are out of our control or reach, and all we can do is pray. Certainly when dealing with the *heart* of man (not his behavior), we are often limited to prayer.

When you and I are in the *unalterable* position where all we can do is pray, then that is what we must do. But when we *can* do more—when we can obey God's commands—to just pray is not only insufficient, it's possibly sin. James said: "Therefore to him that knoweth to do good, and doeth it not, to him it is sin" (4:17). The truth is this: America will not be restored by one glorious prayer meeting, nor one hundred glorious prayer meetings. It will take full obedience, obedience in prayer and action.

Don't Preach the Gospel—Just Pray!

For example, would you give credence to someone who said, "We are no longer going to send money to missionaries. We aren't going to print tracts and Bibles for nations without the Bible; we aren't going to train and send missionaries anymore; we're simply going to pray for the conversion of the heathen and leave it in God's hands."

Would you agree with such foolishness? I hope not. But that is exactly the lie many of us have bought concerning the life and death struggles of our day. "Just pray, and leave it in God's hands!"

Does God want child-killing? Not unless He's schizophrenic. He said, "You shall not murder" (Exod. 20:13). So then why do we have it?

Because the Church allows it! We have the manpower and the resources; we just don't have the will. We've prayed that God would end child-killing, but God has already *commanded us* to "justice . . . defend the orphan, plead for the widow" (Isa. 1:17). God has commanded us to "rescue those who are unjustly sentenced to death" (Prov. 24:11). We need to pray for God's help, wisdom, protection, and provision *and then fight for all we're worth—* not go back into the comfort of our pew or our living room sofa.

The same principle holds true for pornography, the homosexual agenda, condom-pushing in schools, the passing of ungodly federal or state laws, etc.

Consider Goliath. For forty days he derided and blasphemed God and mocked the children of Israel. Undoubtedly, many Israelites held prayer meetings.

I can hear the leaders now. *"Now stretch out your hands, brethren! We rebuke the spirit of Satan over Goliath! We bind him from his mockeries!"*

It didn't work. He kept mocking.

"Oh, God! Do You see him blaspheming? Open up the earth and swallow him as you did Korah in the day of his rebellion!"

The earth isn't hungry.

"Oh, God, we command fire to come down from heaven and consume him as it did in the day of Nadab and Abibu as when they offered up strange fire! Destroy him with the blast of your nostrils!"

Sorry. Mostly blue skies, slightly overcast. Temperatures in the mid-eighties. No barbecued Goliath today.

You see, God was waiting for someone to put feet on his prayers. Yes, He wanted a praying man. Yes, He wanted someone with faith. But that someone had to be willing to go into the battle and confront the enemy face to face. A physical enemy required physical action.

"Then said David to the Philistine, Thou comest to me with a sword, and with a spear, and with a shield: but I come to thee in the name of the LORD of hosts, the God of the armies of Israel, whom thou hast defied. This day will the LORD deliver thee into mine hand; and I will smite thee, and take thine head from thee; and I will give the carcasses of the host of the Philistines this day unto the fowls of the air, and to the wild beasts of the earth;

that all the earth may know that there is a God in Israel. And all this assembly shall know that the LORD saveth not with sword and spear: for the battle *is* the LORD's, and he will give you into our hands" (1 Sam. 17:45-47).

David had great faith, a great confession, an assurance that the battle was the Lord's. What did he do next? Did he go home and listen to contemporary Christian music? No. *He fought* under God's anointing. He used what he had. But it wasn't a magic wand or simply a confession. He had a real sling that threw a real stone, that sunk into a real forehead, and knocked down a real man. He then took Goliath's real sword, and cut off his real head, and made a real bloody mess. No fairy tales here, folks.

David was a man after God's own heart (Acts 13:22). He was a praying man. The Psalms are filled with his prayers and hymn/prayers. But this is how we are introduced to David—as a man of action. David prayed for wisdom, strength, protection, blessing, and then he acted— he fought with all his might. Was David using the "arm of the flesh"? Or was he being an example of what it means to be a man after God's own heart?

Psalm 18 is a divine portrait of the balance between prayer and action. David wrote in verses 1-6:

"I will love thee, O LORD, my strength. The Lord *is* my rock, and my fortress, and my deliverer; my God, my strength, in whom I will trust; my buckler, and the horn of my salvation, *and* my high tower. I will call upon the LORD, *who is worthy* to be praised: so shall I be saved from mine enemies. The sorrows of death compassed me, and the floods of ungodly men made me afraid. The sorrows of hell compassed me about: the snares of death prevented me. In my distress I called upon the LORD, and cried unto my God: he heard my voice out of his temple, and my cry came before him, *even* into his ears."

If you were to read this and stop here, you might have the false impression that David never lifted a finger in battle, that God just did it all. Not so. Look at verses 29-40.

"For by thee **I have run through a troop**; and by my God have I **leaped over a wall**. *As for* God, his way *is* perfect: the word of the Lord is tried: he *is* a buckler to all those that trust in him. For who *is* God save the Lord? Or who *is* a rock save our God? *It is* God that **girdeth me with strength,** and maketh my way perfect. **He maketh my feet** like hinds' *feet*, and setteth me upon my high places. **He teacheth my hands to war,** so that a bow of steel is broken by mine arms. Thou hast also given me the shield of thy salvation: and thy right hand hath holden me up, and thy gentleness hath made me great. Thou hast enlarged my steps under me, that my feet did not slip. **I have pursued mine enemies,** and overtaken them: neither did I turn again till they were consumed. **I have wounded them** that they were not able to rise: they are fallen under my feet. **For thou hast girded me with strength unto the battle:** thou hast subdued under me those that rose up against me. Thou hast also given me the necks of mine enemies; that I might destroy them that hate me" (emphasis added).

By God's strength, David runs through a troop and leaps over a wall. God teaches David's hands to war. God enlarged David's steps so that he wouldn't slip. David didn't just stand there. He pursued his enemies and struck them till they could not rise. David was no harp-playing pew potato!

He prayed as if it all depended on God and fought as if it all depended on him. He was a man of prayer and action, a man after God's own heart. We would do well to follow his example.

Examine your heart and life. Have you been lulled into the magic-wand syndrome? Are you praying, but not fighting?

Over the past twenty years, many prayer "movements," prayer ministries, and prayer seminars have come and gone. Many leaders of these phenomenon have given their followers a false hope that prayer would be enough to turn America around. They have gathered in huge numbers, preached inspiring messages, and prayed fierce prayers. Men and women have then committed to praying in groups and alone, at all hours of the day and night.

Tragically, this prayer energy has often been squandered. Would to God these dear saints had an agenda of action—a battle plan for the reformation of the country that they were praying about. It's one thing to gather and pray about a godless sex-ed curriculum. It's another to pray for two Christians who are running for school board so that the curriculum can be kept (or tossed) out.

It's one thing to pray for righteous government in general prayers. It's another to pray (and work) for a righteous congressman to replace a wicked congressman.

The general, "revival/Oh God, how long" prayer movements have not been sustainable. Why? I'm sure many reasons may exist, but one key reason is that *it isn't* working.

Prayer Is Not Enough

That's right, prayer alone is not enough. Consider the amount of prayer that has been generated by the huge prayer movements in the past twenty years. But the prayer has not been balanced with action. The outcome? We have lost ground on every major front, in every major field of battle. I challenge you to show me one major power base where we have gained ground and not lost ground.

Why? Because prayer is not enough. Prayer is not a magic wand. We cannot be happy, dumb, lazy, and fat and then expect a quick (or long) prayer to resolve the crisis. We cannot pray to God to do what He has commanded us to do.

For example: If a family is starving because the father is lazy and does not provide for his family, he is worse than an infidel (1 Tim. 5:8). The solution for him is not to pray for daily bread; it is for him to repent and work as God has commanded him. Likewise, America is starving for watchmen on the wall, starving for men and women of passion, courage, and integrity to lead us out of this mess. Prayer is critical; we must agonize in prayer at this time. We must pray that from the churches' bosom come the Daniels, the Josephs, the Deborahs, the Josiahs to end the starvation for righteous leaders and lead America out of this mess. And then we must work with them, as the Israelites worked with Nehemiah, to rebuild the walls of righteousness. God grant it! Help us to pray and obey!

The first step in the creation of their [Nazi] new indigenous Church was to get rid of the "Old Testament with its Jewish morality of rewards, and its stories of cattle-dealers and concubines."[1]

It is urgently desired that by the end of the year no more denominational schools or monastic or conventual schools should exist. In many cases it should be possible to carry out these orders by the beginning of the second half of the school year 1939. Further, you should take all other possible steps to remove denominational influences from the German educational system. By the end of the year, no educational institutions should exist which are under denominational influence. Particularly, this includes orphanages, foster homes, boarding-houses and hostels. Only in those places where the Church authorities have an overwhelming proportion of the facilities, such as kindergartens, nursing homes, etc. and where the take-over cannot be effected because of the lack of other resources and the necessary personnel within a short time, should the process be stretched out over a longer period.[2]

Martin Bormann, June 1939

Ten

THE WAR OF
THE TESTAMENTS
(Was Moses Really All That Bad?)

"Is that in the New Testament?"

"When did Jesus *Himself* do that?"

If I hear these questions one more time, I'm going to scream.

These two questions crop up thousands of times a day in conversations, Bible studies, and churches all over America. The theological presuppositions undergirding these questions are error at best and poisonous heresy at worst.

When someone asks the question, "Did Jesus ever do that," they are implying that if Jesus did *not* do "that," then we aren't called to do it either. As I intend to show, this is folly. Jesus never got married and never had children. Do they intend to forbid us to marry, as Paul warned some would? (see 1 Tim. 4:3).

A Christian who asks, "Is that in the New Testament?" is implying that biblical truth from Genesis to Malachi, especially the Pentateuch (Genesis-Deuteronomy), is not binding on us today. Their attitude seems to be, "If it ain't in the New Testament, it ain't for me." This also is severe error. As Gary North poignantly asks: Where in the New Testament is bestiality condemned or prohibited? Certainly the New Testament-only crowd would not say bestiality is now acceptable.

For discussion purposes, I want to break down the questions into two areas:

1) The person of Christ and the nature of God

2) The Old Testament versus the New Testament.

From the onset, let me be very clear: I am going to give a brief overview of the topics in discussion. This chapter is barely an introduction into "Theology 101" and is designed to cause more questions than to give answers. Furthermore, I write about God and the nature of God in the fear of the Lord. I want to flush out faulty theology that has taken up residence in our lives, our churches, our Bible colleges. If I succeed in demolishing some strongholds of error and leave you with a lot of questions, that's okay. Read your Bible!

On to our discussion.

The Life and Teachings of Christ

I absolutely love the Gospels. I've shed many tears of joy over the wonder of the Savior and many tears of remorse for my own sins when I read Matthew, Mark, Luke, and John.

My life has been challenged, instructed, and redirected by reading and meditating on the Sermon on the Mount. I've been overcome by emotion as I've meditated on Christ freeing the demonic. My heart has been smitten as I've read and reread the accounts of Christ's passion. Oh, the wonder. Thank God for the Gospels. We must cherish this historically accurate account of Christ's life.

Tragically, many Christians have made two errors concerning Christ in the Gospels:

1) They extract an unbiblical, out-of-balance view of Jesus from the Gospels.

2) They wrongly believe that Jesus is fully and completely revealed in the Gospels. (He is not.)

I sometimes think that the first group (with the "unbiblical Jesus") imagines Jesus with sandy blond hair and blue eyes, with a distant, mystic look. They follow a Jesus who would never say an unkind or harsh word to anyone, a Jesus so full of love (mush love) that He would never display anger; a Jesus who would never hurt a flea.

This is certainly a poor reading of the Scriptures.

The Jesus who said, "Come to Me all who labor and are heavy laden" (see Matthew 11:28) also said of His people "I . . . will fight against them with the sword of my mouth" (Rev. 2:16).

The Jesus who said turn the other cheek (see Luke 6:29) also overturned tables and came at people with a whip (see John 2:13-17).

The Jesus who said, "Judge not, that ye be not judged" (Matt. 7:1) also said, "But whoso shall offend one of these little ones which believe in me, it were better for him that a millstone were hanged about his neck, and that he were drowned in the depth of the sea" (Matt. 18:6).

The Jesus who told us to love our enemies (see Matthew 5:44) also pronounced the horrifying destruction of Jerusalem—which involved the death of thousands because they rejected Him as Messiah (see Luke 21:20ff).

The Jesus who said, "Go and sin no more" (John 8:11c) also said "I will kill her children with death" (Rev. 2:23).

The Jesus who said, "Greater love hath no man than this, that a man lay down his life for his friends" (John 15:13) also said, "I will spew you out of my mouth" (Rev. 3:16).

Nicer Than Jesus?

I point out these words and actions of Jesus for a dose of theological reality. When studying Christ, we must rightly divide the Word of Truth. Christ's words were not always as nice or kind as we might like. Sometimes they were downright harsh.

Frankly, most Christians today are attempting to be nicer than Jesus. If Christ were in many of our churches or communities today and said some of His more seemingly unkind words, we would probably grab Him, take Him aside, and rebuke Him. "Jesus! You can't talk like that here! We're Christians!" Friend, give up trying to be nicer than Jesus.

The Old God vs. the New God

A far greater problem arises with those who believe that Jesus is fully understood and revealed in the Gospels. This is not accurate. Jesus is revealed from Genesis to Revelation, and the entire Bible must be studied to understand Christ. It is generally agreed that Christ appeared in the Old Testament—occurrences commonly called "Theophonies." And obviously, the Lord is recorded as appearing in the books of Acts and Revelation.

God Is One

God is Father, Son, and Holy Spirit. One God, three persons. Jesus Christ is the same yesterday, today, and forever (Heb. 13:8). There is no shadow of turning with God the Father (James 1:17).

This means that Christ was present in the Godhead when He made the decision to destroy Sodom and Gomorrah and its inhabitants by fire and brimstone (Gen. 19:24). It means that God—Father, Son, and Holy Spirit—commanded Moses and then Joshua to obliterate the reprobate tribes of Canaan.

Millions of Christians have fallen into the theological trap, or at least the theo-emotional trap, that believes that we had one God in the Old Testament and another new God in the New Testament. They see God in the Old Testament as being severe, bordering on mean and unforgiving. Then Jesus comes and saves the day. He gets God the Father to calm down and stop killing people. Ananias and Sapphira were temporary relapses (Acts 5:1-11). And Herod being eaten by worms, well . . . (Acts 12:23).

"Two Gods" is an incorrect, heretical view of God. Yes, God is love (1 John 4:8). God is also Light (1 John 1:5), God is Spirit (John 4:24) , and God is a consuming fire (Heb. 12:29). We've got to reject the notion that Christ and God the Father are at odds with each other between the Testaments.

I want to hasten to say—for balance' sake and because of the innumerable times I have received God's mercy and grace—that God truly is a gracious God, forgiving iniquity and sin (Exod. 20:5-6). I praise God for the atonement of our sins through the blood of Christ, for the fact that Jesus bore the penalty for my sin—death (Rom. 6:23; Isa. 53:4-6). I am not trying to make light of God's unfathomable mercy. I am just trying to make clear that the incredible mercy of God existed before the incarnation, and the severity of God remains after the incarnation. If you doubt the enduring severity of God, take a peek into the Lake of Fire.

This dichotomy of thought about God aids and abets another crippling disease in recent separatist Christianity—theologians call it antinomianism.

We're Not under the Law
(or near it, or in favor of it, or . . .)

You must have heard the annoying question—or perhaps you've asked it: "Is that in the New Testament?"

Perhaps you've quoted a scripture in Deuteronomy or the Proverbs that demands justice, or calls God's people to action, and someone responded with the throwaway line that supposedly ends all debate and relieves us of all responsibility: "That's in the Old Testament."

Millions of misled or deceived Christians discard truth and duty out of hand, solely because they are found between Genesis and Malachi, rather than Matthew and Revelation. (This is a tremendously useful theology for the pew-potato who really doesn't want to act anyway.) The majority of scriptures outlining how a culture should order itself are in the Old Testament. The majority of scriptures demanding we pursue and secure "social" justice and righteousness in society are in the Old Testament. In fact, *most of the Bible* is in the Old Testament. Obeying Old Testament passages that demand we fight for the rights of the oppressed can be a difficult, sometimes thankless task. It's nice to whip out the "get out of

jail duty free" card any time responsibility comes knock-
ing: "That's the Old Testament."

Perhaps some clarity would be in order. I am not in
any way teaching that we can earn righteousness or right
standing with God by works of the law, for "by the works
of the law no flesh will be justified in His sight" (Rom.
3:20). Righteousness is a gift of God (Rom. 5:17) which
comes to us through faith in Christ (Eph. 2:8-9). And I am
certainly not suggesting that we return to full Mosaic
Law, i.e., animal sacrifices, the Aaronic priesthood, the
Levites, etc. Jesus' death was the perfect blood sacrifice
able to atone for the sins of the world. Moreover, He has
made all believers into a royal priesthood. Christ's death
brought an end to the types and shadows.

However, the phrase "we are not under the Law"
(Rom. 6:14-15) has been stretched to the biblical breaking
point. Young Christians and unstudied older Christians
flippantly dismiss sacred truth with that smug answer,
not knowing what it means.

We are not under the Law as a means of obtaining
salvation, and as Christians, we are not under the curse
even though we are still bound by the moral dictates of
the Law, i.e., the Ten Commandments. Jesus said, "Do
not think that I came to abolish the law, or the Prophets:
I did not come to abolish, but to fulfill" (Matt. 5:17). Paul
said, "Do we then nullify the Law through faith? May it
never be! On the contrary, we establish the Law" (Rom.
3:31).

Jesus made it clear when He stated:

"Whosoever therefore shall break one of these least
commandments, and shall teach men so, he shall be called
the least in the kingdom of heaven: but whosoever shall
do and teach them, the same shall be called great in the
kingdom of heaven" (Matt. 5:19).

And then He went on to say:

"Woe unto you, scribes and Pharisees, hypocrites! for
ye pay tithe of mint and anise and cummin, and have
omitted the weightier matters of the law, judgment, mercy,

and faith: these ought ye to have done, and not to leave the other undone" (Matt. 23:23).

Paul wrote, "But we know that the law is good, if a man use it lawfully; knowing this, that the law is not made for a righteous man, but for the lawless and disobedient, for the ungodly and for sinners, for unholy and profane, for murderers of fathers and murderers of mothers, for manslayers" (1 Tim. 1:8-9).

Unfortunately many, if not most, Christians in America have a strong dislike that borders on antipathy for the laws and the punishments of Mosaic Law, as well as the prophetic books announcing God's judgments.

Before you fall into a spiritual fit, let me paint a scenario for you that will vividly illustrate the nature of the problem.

If tomorrow God required all those "hard case" laws, i.e., the stoning of Sabbath-breakers and adulterers, most of us would feel ourselves ill-used. In fact, most Christians would scream bloody murder as if a grave injustice had occurred.

This is the core of the problem. Many in our ranks believe God's justice to be unjust; we believe God's judgments to be unfair. We believe God's punishment to be too severe. Taken one small step further, many of us think God's Laws (and punishments) are unreasonable, unmerciful, or cruel. But the Bible says: "The law of the Lord is perfect, converting the soul: the testimony of the Lord is sure, making wise the simple. The statutes of the Lord are right, rejoicing the heart: the commandment of the Lord is pure, enlightening the eyes. The fear of the Lord is clean, enduring for ever: the judgments of the Lord are true and righteous altogether. More to be desired are they than gold, yea, than much fine gold: sweeter also than honey and the honeycomb. Moreover by them is thy servant warned: and in keeping of them there is great reward" (Ps. 19:7-11).

Unfortunately, it seems many Christians would disagree.

Heaven help us if we as Christians who love God and say we believe His Word is inspired and infallible should turn around and say that His Laws are unjust.

"But wait!" some will say. "Jesus gave us a new law—the law of love." True, Jesus said the duty of man was to love God with all his heart, soul, mind, and strength, and to love his neighbor as himself (Matt. 22:37, 39). Why? "On these two commandments hang all the law and the prophets" (Matt. 22:40). Christ's commands to love God and man were summarizing God's requirements of man—not replacing them. Unless you know the Law and the Prophets, you won't know the means of expressing your love to God and man.

The Law and the Gospel

Those self-assured Christians who throw out the Law and smugly declare that they only "preach grace" are fools. I believe one major reason we have so few real, lasting conversions today is because we don't preach the Law before we preach grace.

People in sin need a Savior. How does someone know he is in sin? "I would not have come to know sin except through the Law" (Rom. 7:7). What brings men to Christ is the Law, the schoolmaster. "Wherefore the law was our schoolmaster *to bring us* unto Christ, that we might be justified by faith" (Gal. 3:24).

"But wait!" you might venture. "Once we are saved, we no longer need the law. We're under the new covenant."

True, we are under a glorious new covenant sealed in Divine blood. But part of the New Covenant is the promise of God to write the law on our hearts. "After those days, saith the Lord, I will put my law in their inward parts, and write it in their hearts; and will be their God, and they shall be my people" (Jer. 31:33). Why would we try and dismiss what God wants to write on our hearts?

Are You Properly Equipped?

If you don't know the Law, if you are not a student of the Old Testament, you will flounder at best, ever being an out-of-balance Christian without sure moorings. Your doctrine will be the poorer, you will be in much need of reproof and correction, and you will not be properly equipped for the Lord's work. In the great fields of labor that lie before us, you will be at best a second-rate worker in the field.

How can I be so sure? Because the Bible says so.

"All Scripture is given by inspiration of God, and is profitable for doctrine, for reproof, for correction, for instruction in righteousness: that the man of God may be perfect, thoroughly furnished unto all good works" (2 Tim. 3:16-17).

When Paul wrote this the only scripture they had was the Old Testament! The printing of the New Testament *adds* to the Scriptures, it doesn't *take away*.

If you truly want balanced doctrine, you must know the whole Bible; if you earnestly desire the reproof of God in your life for what displeases Him, or if you want to rebuke the wicked, you must know Genesis to Revelation. If you intend to bring correction to families, schools, churches, businesses, government agencies, and the judiciary, you must know the Old Testament as well as the New Testament.

And yet so many Christians glibly dismiss Mosaic Law, the Psalms, the Proverbs, the Prophets, by asking, "Is it in the New Testament?" Enough of this!

I was recently on a Christian radio show in California where a Christian sister was interviewing me (or should I say abusing me). I was explaining to her and the listeners that as Christians, we have a duty to try and save children from abortion and to fight to end abortion in America.

She pompously demanded of me, "But where did *Jesus* say we have to rescue someone?" She really thought she had me stumped.

Think this through with me. A radio talk show host who regularly speaks to hundreds of Christians—perhaps thousands—believes that unless Jesus said we have to rescue people, we don't have to rescue anyone. "Let those staggering toward death die!" (Compare that with Proverbs 24:10-12.) Perhaps she never read the story of the Good Samaritan.

I explained to her that Jesus helped inspire the whole Bible and that our Christian duty is revealed from Genesis to Revelation. She abandoned that line of attack very quickly.

Check Your Pockets

Friend, have you been robbed? Have the theological escapists and the New Testament-only crowd robbed you of your "equipment"? The whole Bible is the Sword of the Spirit. We don't want to go into battle with three-quarters of our sword broken off!

The theological challenge before us is not to throw the baby out with the bath water. Obviously, portions of the Pentateuch are no longer to be practiced today because Christ has come. Obviously, our justification before God is through faith—although faith without works is dead (James 2:26). Obviously, certain portions of the Law have been superseded by New Testament revelation and teaching.

For example, there are New Testament reasons why we don't stone adulterers and Sabbath-breakers. (I would encourage you to dig them out for yourself.)

I know I've created tension in some hearts, and you may have a dozen questions about particulars. This is not the place I will answer them, nor am I certain I could answer every question. In fact, I'm 100 percent sure I could *not* answer every question! This type of thinking certainly required more thought and study than the wholesale rejection of the Old Testament.

I am not trying to give all the answers. I'm asking questions. If the church has a log in its eye—a dislike that borders on contempt for the Law—how can we ever hope to remove the splinters out of this culture's eye, i.e., the culture's rejection of the Bible? What have we become when those of us who should love the Word of God are repulsed by portions of it? What evil force has overcome us when we look suspiciously at *fellow Christians* who promote the Law of God? Something is dreadfully wrong, dear friend, when the enemies of God mock the Old Testament, and the people of God concur that "those laws were for a different culture" or "those laws were only for ancient Israel, not for today." God save us from trite, pat answers, and God save us from trying to make the awesome, fearful commands of our God palatable to rebellious man.

We must studiously examine the Scriptures in the fear of the Lord. We must reject the simplistic notion that if it's in the Old Testament, it's not for today. We must reject the concept that God changed in nature between the Old and New Testaments. We must study and live the whole Bible, applying the clear meaning of biblical law when we can—such as calling for the execution of murderers. We must apply the principles of biblical Law when the specific Law no longer has direct application—such as Mosaic building codes to protect people on the second floor from falling through the ceiling. Or consider the principle of separating—quarantining—those with a deadly disease. (Those with tuberculosis have always been quarantined. Why haven't we protected innocent people from AIDS carriers in some manner?)

In the light of the whole counsel of God, we will be equipped for service and battle in our culture, and we will be able to provide *biblical* solutions to all of man's problems (economic problems, political problems, education problems, medical problems, judicial problems, restitution problems) because the Bible addresses them all—flawlessly.

Speaking of political problems, we need to look intently into the Word of God concerning the role and *lim-*

ited sphere of government in the Bible. The Bible teaches that government should have a very limited role. It should not be the ever-expanding, messianic provider/healer that the Marxist/Socialists have created in much of Europe, Canada, and now America.

I'll take the standards, warnings, and solutions God gave to Moses or King David, King Solomon or the Prophets, over anything that Bill Clinton, Ted Kennedy, or a pagan Supreme Court could ever offer.

We have brought the priests out of the Party political conflict, and led them back into the Church. And now it is our desire that they should never return to that area for which they were not intended.[1]

Adolf Hitler, 24 October 1933

Most Church leaders, were anxious to keep their Church intact and at the same time, at whatever cost to their theological principles, to support the new regime. But for the Nazis that was not enough. The only sphere in which they were prepared to tolerate Church activity was in purely "spiritual" matters concerned with the next world. The separation of Church and State was designed to drive churchmen out of every public activity.[2]

Eleven

BATTLING
IN HOUSTON
(Jezebel vs. The Prophets)

"So long as no direct attempt was made to interfere with the ministrations of Word and Sacrament, many of the Bishops and the clergy were content to leave political affairs to the Nazis."[3]

The days of unfettered liberty for preaching the whole counsel of God, and even "the gospel" (as we discussed in chapter 6), are drawing to a close.

The double tragedy of the separatist escapists is not only that they have little impact on the pagan culture at large, but they are in danger even in their fox-holes. The pagans in powerful governmental positions will not be content to leave them alone to preach the Word in public, to fellow Christians, and even behind church doors.

As you will see, God-hating judges, the Internal Revenue Service, and various legislative bodies are using the same arguments as Hitler and the Nazis to stamp out the Word of God, usurp its authority, and to subvert its influence in every aspect of public life.

Consider this: A public school teacher cannot recite the 23rd Psalm to his class, but he can tell your son where to get a condom or your daughter an abortion without your knowledge or consent. Your tax dollars are hard at work. In fact—as you know—your tax dollars regularly pay for blasphemy against Christ through the National Endowment for the Arts.

Remember, we are in a cultural civil war, and our enemies want total dominion. And they are bent on crushing dissent. Those in government who view the state as the Messiah are compelled to eliminate all rival deities.

Houston

In August of 1992, during the Republican National Convention in Houston, Operation G. O. P. (Guard Our Pre-born) took place. The child-killers went to court and found a willing feminist activist judge to do their bidding.

The judge issued what until that time was the most tyrannical order I had ever seen concerning pro-life activism and free speech.

It read in part:

> It is therefore ORDERED: the defendants, their officers, directors, agents and representatives, and all other persons, known or unknown, acting in their behalf or in concert with them, are restrained and enjoined until the hearing of the State's Application for Temporary Injunction from doing any of the following:
>
> . . . 2. Demonstrating within one-hundred (100) feet from either side of or in front of any doorway entrance, parking lot or parking lot entrance, driveway or driveway entrance of any such health care facility in Harris County or the City of Houston;
>
> 3. Demonstrating within twenty-five (25) feet of any person seeking access to or leaving any such health care facility or its parking lot, or in any way impeding such person's entrance to or exit from such facility or parking lots in Harris County or the City of Houston;
>
> . . . 6. Making any sound or noise (whether by mechanical loudspeakers, sound amplification device, or otherwise) that is so loud that it disturbs, injures,

or endangers their health or safety of any patient or employee of any health care facility at which abortions are performed in Harris County or the City of Houston.

Preaching Christ Equals "Demonstrating"

What made this order so blatantly evil was that Judge O'Neill construed *any Christian actions*—whether quietly picketing or preaching about Jesus or even kneeling and praying—as being "demonstrations." On 18 August 1992, Reverend Patrick Mahoney, Reverend Phillip Benham, Bob Jewitt, and Wendy Wright were across the street from Planned Parenthood, on a *public sidewalk*, praying, talking, and preaching the gospel. Reverend Benham is a long-time street preacher, and he was preaching Christ to the lost. He also quietly approached some women seeking abortion and offered them help to carry their babies to term.

Judge O'Neill dragged them before her bench and found them in contempt of court. She locked up all four until they paid a five hundred dollar fine and promised in open court to obey her godless order. They all refused. (They ended up serving twenty-one days.)

Heartache unto Death

To give you an idea of how vexingly unjust her "court" was, I give you this story. In the middle of the proceedings, which lasted several days, Father Joe O'Gara, a Catholic priest, came in from California. He was a dear man, a quiet but ardent pro-lifer, and a seasoned rescuer. I had known him for three years. After his first day in court as an observer, he emerged from the proceedings with tears in his eyes, stricken with grief over the injustice.

We proceeded to the evening rally and when it was over, we asked him to close the meeting in prayer. He prayed thoughtfully and emotionally. He was so distraught, and his blood pressure was so elevated, that a blood vessel burst in his brain. (We didn't know it at the time.) He complained when he sat down after praying that he was disoriented. His heart rate was very high, and his face very red. We prayed with him and called an ambulance which came right away. As they wheeled him out on the stretcher, I rubbed his arm, and we said good-bye with smiles, believing we would see each other again very soon.

That night, he fell into a deep coma. Jeff White, Joe Slovenic, and I went to the hospital and stood by his side, praying, trying to comfort him spiritually (if his soul and spirit could hear or sense us). It was gut-wrenching. We had to fight with the hospital to keep feeding him, no matter what. It didn't matter much. He never regained consciousness, and he died within forty-eight hours.

This is part of the legacy of Judge Eileen O'Neill.

The Local Clergy Arise

The anguish and anger felt by that dear priest were felt by clergy throughout the city. Those who came to the proceedings were dumbfounded by the tyranny and injustice in O'Neill's court.

Then a miracle of courage took place. The local pastors and ministers recognized that O'Neill's injunction was a direct assault on the freedom to preach the gospel. They sounded the alarm to their congregations and prepared to flood the streets with people.

I have never experienced anything like it. The sense of destiny we shared, the passion and vision that constrained us were truly compelling. This tyrant-judge was seeking to stop the preaching of the gospel, and these men of God were not going to bow the knee. I cannot express to you in words the joy I felt as dozens of ministers stepped forward, absolutely determined to stand for God's Word, even if it meant going to jail. I have never seen anything like the resolve and the singleness of purpose they shared. It was truly a historic moment (deserving an entire book, not just a chapter in one!).

When the first morning of mass defiance arrived, dozens of clergy were joined by hundreds of Houston Christians inside O'Neill's "gospel-free zone." We were blessed to be joined by Dr. Dobson's cousin, Reverend Herb London. He laughingly said he was being "pushed toward the bullets." We were glad to have him.

The ministers one by one stepped on a ladder, took up a bullhorn, and preached the gospel. They also stated clearly they were doing it "in conjunction with Operation Rescue" (which further defied the order). Joe Slovenic and I also participated in these excursions—when Joe and I preached, the pro-death leaders asked the hundreds of pro-death activists to be quiet so they could clearly capture our actions and words on video and then take them to the judge so we would be held in contempt and put in jail. We were able to boldly preach the gospel to hundreds of lost souls and solemnly warn them of the danger of judgment they were in.

When all the pastors had preached, we went to the court en masse. The clergy politely insisted to the killers' attorneys that they be put in jail also!

The killers' attorneys and the judge were shocked, and none of the pastors were jailed.

The clergy went a step further. Pastor Phil Arms had the great idea to take out a full-page advertisement in the *Houston Post* declaring their righteous defiance to the judge. Pastor Ernie Fitzpatrick and I hammered out a rough draft. A few other men made touch-ups.

Here is the text:

JUDGE EILEEN O'NEILL

190th District Court

We the following pastors and ministers of Houston, Texas, do hereby

DEFY YOUR INJUNCTION

and challenge you to place us in JAIL along with the other Christians who are NOW IN JAIL because of your capricious and illegal order which makes it a CRIME if:

1. We pray on any street or sidewalk within 100 feet of an abortuary.

2. We preach the Gospel of Jesus Christ within 100 feet of an abortuary.

This is a flagrant violation of our First Amendment rights. The STATE has no right to tell pastors and ministers of the Word of God where we can and cannot pray or preach on a public sidewalk.

Hence, we hereby pledge as servants of Christ to actively, knowingly, and willfully pray and preach the Gospel outside area abortuaries in spite of your injunction!

Let Our Fellow Ministers Go, OR PUT US ALL IN JAIL!

(Included in the advertisement were the signatures of sixty ministers representing numerous different churches.)

After the advertisement ran, they continued to go to the Planned Parenthood mill en masse. Pastor Joe Slovenic and I joined them. The judge then "requested" the presence of Reverend Joe Slovenic, Jeff White, and myself before her for our part in these activities.

Before long, Reverend Slovenic and I were off to jail to join our friends. We ended up staying in jail five days for preaching the gospel *across the street* from a Planned Parenthood abortion mill.

Advocates to the Rescue

We were all released from jail after Jay Sekulow and other staff attorneys from the A. C. L. J. (American Center for Law and Justice) came to Houston. They filed emergency *habeas corpus* motions in the local state court which were denied. They then went to the Supreme Court of Texas, the highest court. The justices saw the illegality of Judge O'Neill's order, and we were released immediately. I can only hope someday she spends two days in jail for every day she jailed Christians for preaching and praying. That would be just restitution.

You would think O'Neill would have backed down after being humbled by the Supreme Court of Texas. But her arrogance and her blind commitment to child-killing seemed to drive her. She altered slightly her order but maintained a gospel-free zone. The local clergy have continued to obey God and defy her, and as of this writing almost one year later, nothing has been done to them. Babies are being rescued, and souls are being saved. A few weeks ago, Planned Parenthood's security guard became a Christian and quit Planned Parenthood. Would to God this type of conviction would capture the clergy and the whole church nationwide!

We Nazis demand a separation of Church and State in the entire public life of the country. What is the sense in still having Catholic associations of civil servants? We do not want Protestant or Catholic civil servants, we want German civil servants. What is the point of the Catholic Daily Press? We do not need a Catholic or a Protestant but only a German Press. The Catholic professional organizations and the Catholic youth organizations no longer fit into our age. They are often active in areas which the Nazi State claims for itself in fulfillment of its tasks. All these things are designed to disturb the unity of the German people, which Adolf Hitler created after fifteen years of struggle for the soul of Germany.[1]

Wilhelm Frick, Minister of the Interior

Against the Nazis' secret practice of euthanasia, which was gradually becoming known, and the public propaganda in favour of sexual promiscuity, regrettably few Churchmen raised their voices; and, indeed, few seemed to understand that such practices presented a fundamental challenge to Christian thought and doctrine.[2]

It will be apparent in the coming weeks whether the Catholics will possess enough sense to give up of their own accord this freakish and disloyal system of theirs or whether it will be necessary to use force. . . . And unless the devil himself is against us, we shall succeed in compelling the Catholics just as we have compelled the hundred and one other clubs and associations.[3]

Baldur von Schirach, 9 April 1935

Twelve

BATTLING
WITH CONGRESS
(Criminals Making the Laws)

Before Bill Clinton became president, he promised to "move against the anti-choice extremists who have block-aded family planning clinics across the country. Appearances by these groups, including Operation Rescue, at nearly every stop Al Gore and I made on our 'First 1,000 Miles' bus tour show their clear intent: to stop the wheels of change and to destroy freedom of choice for women" (Bill Clinton fund-raising letter of 10 August 1992).

His election, coupled with the killing of abortionist David Gunn, spurred a fresh wave of political hysteria to turn certain pro-life activities into a federal offense.

Here are parts of the proposed legislation:

S 248. Blocking access to clinic entrances

(a) Whoever, with intent to prevent or discourage any person from obtaining reproductive health services, intentionally and physically obstructs, hinders, or impedes the ingress or egress of another to a medical facility that affects interstate commerce, or to the structure or place in which the medical facility is located, shall be subject to the penalties provided in sub (b) of this section and the civil remedy provided in subsection (c) of this section.

(b) The penalty for an offense under subsection (a) of this section is a fine under this title, or imprisonment—

(1) for not more than one year, in the case of a first conviction under this section; and

(2) for not more than three years, in the case of an offender who has been convicted of a previous offense under this section; or both such fine and imprisonment.

(c)(1) A qualified plaintiff may in a civil action obtain appropriate relief with respect to any violation of subsection (a) of this section. [That means they can sue us.]

The amount of potential fine is still being debated (it has ranged from one thousand to two hundred and fifty thousand dollars).

While the bill was still in sub-committee, I was called upon to testify before Congress along with Reverend Joe Foreman, Jeff White, and Kathy Hudson. The following was my prepared opening statement:

Statement of Randall A. Terry
To House Sub-Committee on Crime
April 1, 1993

Ladies and Gentlemen, thank you for the opportunity of testifying before you today.

I founded Operation Rescue in 1987 with the express desire of calling the church and the nation to repentance for our national sin of child killing, euphemistically known as abortion. One of the many fruits of repentance for this holocaust is for individuals to nonviolently place their body between the child and the would-be killers. Operation Rescue participants are required to make a commitment to non-violence. To date, over 60,000 arrests have taken place in the past 5 years, perhaps making Operation Rescue the largest civil disobedience movement in American history.

What is the profile of the average rescuer? It defies pigeonholing, except to say all are unalterably opposed to child killing. We believe abortion is murder.

Many are grandmothers, quietly praying with rosaries. Many are young women with young children of their own. Thousands of God-fearing, law-abiding clergy have been arrested with us—Catholic, Protestant and Orthodox—as well as Jewish Rabbis. Multitudes of dads and grandfathers—responsible men in the community—including business owners, firemen, doctors, lawyers, and yes, even policemen have participated in these activities.

To in any way label this diverse cross section of Americans as violent terrorists—as our opposition often does—is to betray the meaning of the word "terrorism" and insults the families of those who have died at the hands of real terrorists.

It is important to note that the normal charge against our activists is simple trespass, disorderly conduct, or failure to disperse. At times we have been charged with resisting arrest for going limp, requiring arresting officers to carry activists, but not for attempting to assault officers. Moreover, I am not aware of any conviction for any violence or assault by a pro-lifer at an Operation Rescue event. To the contrary, the peaceful composure with which pro-lifers have carried themselves while being systematically tortured by police, or kicked, punched, and spit upon by pro-abortion activists is simply astounding.

Along with the brutal treatment many pro-lifers have endured at the hand of certain law enforcement agencies—the LAPD being the worst offender to date—we have already been subjected to incredibly harsh jail sentences for our actions. Hundreds in our ranks have spent multiple months, even years, behind bars for peacefully sitting in front of a door, while repeat drug offenders were, and are, being set free. However, the real revelation of injustice against pro-lifers is seen when comparing the criminal sentences given our people with that of other "civil disobedience" activists.

Before going further, let me make one thing clear—I understand the difference between "First Amendment" protected speech, and "civil disobedience." And

I understand that the behavior in discussion would arguably not fall under current First Amendment protected activities.

However, America enjoys a rich heritage of political speech and activism known as "civil disobedience" in the tradition of Rev. Dr. King and Mahatma Ghandi. From Susan B. Anthony to Rosa Parks, from Levi Coffin (of the underground railroad) to Dr. King— who we celebrate as a national hero, we have a rich heritage of courageous men and women who peacefully challenged man's existing laws to uphold the justice of a Higher Law. Dr. King's letter from the Birmingham Jail is probably the most eloquent and concise defense of civil disobedience ever written. I patterned much of Operation Rescue's literature, training, and tactics after the civil disobedience practiced by civil rights activists of the sixties.

Our nation's very birth was an act of civil disobedience, undergirded by the belief that God, not the state, had endowed men with certain inalienable rights, the right to life being paramount.

Having said that, consider the leniency extended to other activist groups:

• In Washington, D.C., activists against apartheid, including congressmen, sat in at the South African Embassy. They were arrested. They were fined $50 and that was the end of the matter. In comparison, I and several associates are being fined hundreds of thousands of dollars for peacefully sitting-in at a D.C. area abortion facility.

• In New York City, homosexuals sat in at St. Patrick's Cathedral, disrupted the Mass and desecrated the Eucharist. They were very loud, extremely vulgar and blasphemous. They were arrested and released. Their punishment? A $100 fine. In comparison, pro-lifers have been fined hundreds of thousands of dollars because of sit-ins outside N.Y. City abortion facilities.

• In the Los Angeles area, nuclear energy and arms protesters are regularly arrested for sit-ins at nuclear power facilities and military bases. After actor Martin

Sheen was arrested for the eighteenth time, he was given a small fine and community service. In comparison, rescuers in the L.A. area, following their first arrest for a peaceful sit-in, were being sentenced to weeks and even months in jail. These inequities are outrageous.

Will AIDS activists who obstruct access to federal buildings be charged with a federal offense? Will animal rights activists face felony charges for sitting in at a research laboratory? Will homeless advocates be charged with a federal offense for sitting in at a politician's office? Will the library lovers, who recently sat in here in a D.C. area library to oppose the shorter hours, be granted extended reading time via a federal prison sentence? I doubt it.

Let me also point out that several congressmen have been arrested for acts of civil disobedience before or during their tenure. I could continue with other causes, like environmental activists, etc., but I believe the point is clear. The fact is, we are being singled out because we have dared to stand up and fight against the crown-jewel of the politically correct—child killing.

Our opponents have argued that Operation Rescue does not fall into the category of civil disobedience. This hollow argument really means that Operation Rescue is not politically correct civil disobedience.

We must remember, pro-lifers are not the new kid on the block, the abortionists are. Child killing has been illegal in America for over one hundred years prior to *Roe*, and would never have been tolerated by our founding fathers. Most importantly, God has stated clearly in the sixth commandment that "Thou shalt not murder."

Will the death movement's frenzied promotion of child killing blind this investigative body to the obvious? I fear it may but I pray otherwise. The children are victims of murder. Their mothers are being exploited. Their would-be rescuers are the victims of a calculated, political witchhunt.

Ladies and gentlemen, the very introduction of this legislation strikes at the core of what it means to live in political freedom—the right to vigorously disagree, and to non-violently express that dissent—without fear of crushing reprisals from an oppressive government.

I beg you to immediately desist pursuing the Freedom of Access to Clinic Entrance Act.

Once our statements were given, we settled in for over an hour of hostile questioning. Congressman Schumer is the chairman of the subcommittee. Here are some excerpts of the give and take:

Mr. SCHUMER. The hearing will come to order.

Now we are up to Mr. Glickman.

Mr. GLICKMAN. Thank you. Let me ask this question of Mr. Terry, Mr. White, Reverend Foreman, try to answer it as quickly as you can. Do you believe that as the law currently is, that abortion as defined and limited by the Supreme Court is a constitutionally protected right?

Mr. TERRY. Absolutely not. Abortion is the murder of innocent children, and it is not protected.

Mr. GLICKMAN. Under the Constitution as has been interpreted by the Supreme Court. I am not saying you agree with it. I understand you are trying to change it, but I am just asking you, do you accept the fact that it is a constitutionally protected right?

Mr. TERRY. No, I do not, any more than I would have if I had been a Northerner [concerning] slaves when the Supreme Court ruled in Dred Scott that a black man was chattel property. I would refuse to accept it as a constitutional right.

Mr. GLICKMAN. Basically you then say you selectively pick, you believe in some natural law, you don't believe that what the court says as interpreting the Constitution creates a protected right, then? That is an important point.

Mr. TERRY. Very good point, Mr. Glickman. Let me

answer it very concisely. God gave Moses the Ten Commandments. The Ten Commandments must be the foundation of this republic. If they are not, then we will have laws and lawmakers who are blasphemous; idolatrous; lazy; stealing; adulterating; no offense to certain members of the Senate, people who are making laws in this culture.

Mr. GLICKMAN. I understand that, and I understand what you are saying. But again I point out, do you believe that—you may disagree with the nature of the law, but then you do not believe that abortion is a constitutionally protected right as interpreted by the Supreme Court; that is all I am asking.

Mr. TERRY. Was there a factual decision called *Roe v. Wade* where the court said that women have the right to kill their offspring? Of course there was. But do we acknowledge it as binding or valid? Absolutely not.

Mr. GLICKMAN. Okay. But then you believe there is a higher law over and above that?

Mr. TERRY. The Ten Commandments, of course.

Mr. GLICKMAN. The reason why I am saying that is quite honestly, obviously you would recognize it if we selectively in this country decided which laws to obey and which laws not to obey, we face the consequences from that, and you have done that, right?

Mr. TERRY. Of course.

Mr. GLICKMAN. So you don't like the law, you are not—you would like to influence a changing of the law. You don't believe people should obey the law, but you do understand that it is the law, that is why you are engaging—

Mr. TERRY. That is why we get arrested.

. . . .

Mr. TERRY. If I may make one quick point, very quick. We agree that we do not want social anarchy, but the issue in question is not whether or not we pay taxes or not, not whether or not we go to certain facilities, it is a life and death issue.

. . . [Later]

Mr. SCHIFF. What about what has been called generally stalking, and defining that as a problem, anti-stalking statutes. But it has been generally described as following someone on a regular basis on an extended basis everywhere they go with the intent of intimidating them as to what you are going to do next, making your presence known.

. . . .

Mr. TERRY. The doctors who have turned into assassins want to still be respected in the community. They don't want people picketing at their golf club, for example, saying, you know, "Don't hit the club with Dr. So-and-so, he might have used that hand to kill a child this morning." They hate that. It is speech.

We want to know where he plays golf, we want to embarrass him, and if he were really committed to what he was doing, he wouldn't be embarrassed. They do these kinds of things to me constantly. When I was in Florida a week and a half ago, the police came, they said there is a man who said he is coming over with a hand grenade to blow up in this building, in this church. It goes with the turf, but I didn't blink and I didn't back down.

I am not ashamed and they can put my name on all the things they want. They can come to where I play golf and they can mock me until the day I die, and all it does is strengthen my resolve because I know I am right. And if they feel that way, then they shouldn't be intimidated by the fact that they are being exposed in the community. They should be happy that they murdered the innocent for money.

. . . .

Mr. EDWARDS. Well, both Mr. Terry and—well, Mr. Terry said, "I know I am right, I know I am right." Now, how do you know you are right?

Mr. TERRY. Because the eternal law of God that He gave to Moses said: Thou shalt not murder, and wicked men throughout—

Mr. EDWARDS. God told you you are right?

Mr. TERRY. No, Exodus, chapter 20, sir.

Mr. WHITE. Science. If I was not a Christian, if I was a heathen, I would see it the same way because science will prove it.

Mr. EDWARDS. I asked Mr. Terry, he said I know I am right, and he just told me that Moses said he was right. Now, did God tell you you are right, Mr. Terry?

Mr. WHITE. You are trying to mock Mr. Terry, and the truth of the matter is men throughout history—

Mr. EDWARDS. No, I am not. I am asking him a question. He said he knows he is right.

Mr. TERRY. That is correct, sir. I know that murder is wrong.

Mr. EDWARDS. I am asking why he knows he is right, and he said Moses is involved.

Mr. TERRY. God—sir, I am sorry [that he doesn't understand], let me explain to you very clearly. God will hold you and every member of this council accountable for the bloodshed that you are promoting. His law is eternal. You may get away with it until the day you die, but this Nation will pay the price for the bloodshed and you, sir, will also stand before a holy God for your part in the shedding of innocent blood.

As you can see, it was intense from start to finish. I believe God wants to open many doors for Christian leaders to prophecy the Word of God to the ungodly "powers that be," before we replace them with godly leaders.

As Psalm 2 says, "Be wise now therefore O ye kings: be instructed, ye judges of the earth. Serve the Lord with fear, and rejoice with trembling. Kiss the Son, lest he be angry, and ye perish from the way" (verses 10–11).

God give us the courage to speak His Word without compromise.

And on the heights we have planted
The banners of our revolution.
You had imagined that that was all that we
wanted
We want more
We want *all*
Your hearts are our goal,
It is your souls we want.

Anonymous Nazi Verse, 1939[1]

The Nazi interpretation of the slogan "Politics do not belong in the Church" was far more comprehensive and more damaging to the Churches' interests than was realized by the well-meaning churchmen who had agreed to accept it in principle. The slogan had been deliberately coined to conceal the Nazis' intention of excluding the Church from involvement in any aspect of political life.[2]

The bishops' failure to call a spade a spade, their attempts to trade on the popularity of certain Nazi ideas, their continued admonishments to clergy and faithful to not criticize State and Party certainly were little suited to instill anti-Nazi sentiment in their followers. . . . In failing to defend not only the liberty of the Church, but human liberty itself . . . the bishops had inadvertently doomed the chances of winning the struggle against their oppressors.[3]

Thirteen

BATTLING WITH CLINTON

(Betrayal in the Camp)

In the fall of 1992, it became apparent not only that Bill Clinton might win the election, but that millions of Christians might betray the clear teachings of the Bible and vote for him. I believe to do so was sin. (Before you throw down your book, hear me out.)

Our biblical position was simple: If a man has clearly stated that his objective is to break God's commandments (i.e., funding murder, promoting sexual perversion), and someone knowingly helps him in that goal, his accomplice in rebellion is sinning. Bill Clinton had repeatedly stated his wicked goals. He promised to fight for child-killing. He vowed to try and mainline sodomy. Christians who voted for him because of the "economy" put money ahead of God's Word. They were bought off, plain and simple. And Jesus said we cannot serve God and money (Matt. 6:24). (Moreover, God will smash the very idol we bowed to—the economy will crash.)

So, I wrote the tract *Christian Beware: To Vote for Bill Clinton Is to Sin against God.* Christians co-produced and distributed it all over the nation—perhaps 1 1/2 million copies. Soon after the tract was released, our church ran a full-page advertisement warning Christians not to partake of another man's sins.

The advertisement read as follows:

Christian Beware

Do Not Put the Economy Ahead
of the Ten Commandments.
Did you know that Governor Bill Clinton . . .

- **Supports abortion on demand?**
        (Violates Exodus 20:13, Leviticus 20:1-5)
- **Supports the homosexual lifestyle, and wants homosexuals to have special rights?**
        (Violates Exodus 20:14, Leviticus 20:13.
        See also Romans 1:26,27)
- **Promotes giving condoms to teenagers in public
schools?**
        (Violates Exodus 20:12, Colossians 3:5.
        See also Romans 1:28-32)

Bill Clinton is promoting policies that are in rebellion to God's
Laws. In our desire for change, do we really want as a president
and a role model for our children a man of this character who
supports this type of behavior?

But what about the economy?

Yes, we are in tough economic times, *but God forbid that we
sell out our most sacred beliefs in a vain hope of financial gain.*
How can we expect God to bless our economy if we plunge down
a path of immorality? (Deuteronomy 28).

**The Bible warns us to not follow another man in his sin,
nor help him promote sin—lest God chasten *us*.**
        (See Deuteronomy 13, Jeremiah 23,
        Proverbs 4:l4; 11:21; 16:5, I Timothy 5:22)

How then can we vote for Bill Clinton?

As you can see, it was directly addressed to Christians. And the items under discussion are clearly related to biblical ethics and Christianity. Unfortunately, not enough Christians heeded the warning of the flyer and the newspaper advertisement. I've read various polls and each one clearly showed that millions of evangelicals—not to mention Roman Catholics—cast their vote for a man who was blatantly promoting rebellion against God. Had the evangelical community *not* voted for Clinton, he would not have become our forty-second president.

How could so many Christians have been so foolish and so deceived? Bill Clinton said he was saved, he quoted a few Bible verses, and then he promised to get them more money, so they voted for him. They were happier with a godless Baptist who deceptively spoke the lingo, than an Episcopalian who was not fluent in evangelise.

Clinton blatantly promised to promote murder, homosexual abominations, and condom distribution—hence, fornication—to teen–agers. But that did not stop millions of separated Christians (or should I call them morally impaired Christians?) from voting Clinton. They were saved. He said he was saved. He promised their wallet would be saved—that was enough.

Once Clinton took office, he brought with him a cadre of God-hating activists, Socialists, earth worshippers, and the like. And believe me, they are people with an agenda and a vision—and harassing you is a part of their plan.

The day before Clinton's inauguration, 19 January 1993, we ran the following full-page advertisement in Washington in the *Washington Times*:

Mr. Clinton, please do not mock God's Word at your inauguration.

As you know, General George Washington began the tradition of placing one hand on the Sacred Scriptures during the swearing of the oath of office. That Holy Bible plainly teaches that:

- **God hates the shedding of innocent blood,
  such as abortion**
- **Homosexuality is an abomination**
- **Fornication is sin**
- **Those nations which promote such wickedness
  will incur the judgement of God.**

During your campaign, and since your election, you have brazenly committed to promote and aid behavior that is proscribed by Almighty God in His Sacred Word.

Mr. Clinton, for your own sake, repent. Repent of your plans to promote sin against God. If you refuse, do not profane the name of God, nor His Law, by placing your hand on the Scriptures you have no intention of honoring. To do so is a mockery—and God will not be mocked.

THE RESISTANCE

"THOSE WHO FORSAKE THE LAW
                    PRAISE THE WICKED
BUT THOSE WHO KEEP THE LAW
                    RESIST THEM."

—Proverbs 28:4—

The Resistance—P.O. Box 75168—Washington DC 20013

Clinton has obviously ignored biblical advice.

Uncle Pagan Wants You!

The pagan oppressors are after you. You may think they are just after me and a few annoying Christian leaders, but *they are after all of us*. They have you, your family, your church, your neighborhood *squarely* in their sights.

You may think that if you do not associate with a few radicals, you can keep out of the firing line, but you are sadly mistaken. They will not be satisfied until they have crushed all opposition, and everyone has bowed the knee ("Seig Heil!") to their new-world agenda.

They utterly reject the notion that our culture, our laws, our families should be structured according to the Ten Commandments. In fact, they are actively subverting God's commandments (in the name of pluralism, of course).

Do you doubt me? Consider their agenda and their belief system.

Break All Ten Commandments—Flagrantly!

They utterly reject the Lord Jesus Christ as the Savior of sinful mankind and reject the God of the Bible as the only true God. (Violates First Commandment)

Many of them promote pan-theism, new-age spiritism. They bow to the idol of mother earth, animals, and creatures. (Violates Second Commandment)

They mockingly insist on us paying for blasphemy that parades as art; they promote curriculum in schools that undermines faith in God; they use God's and Christ's name in vain in their movies, their television shows, and any other time they feel moved to irreverence. (Violates Third Commandment)

God said "six days shalt thou labor," yet they promote laziness through welfare programs that encourage idleness—and then they steal our money, in the name of compassion, and give it to those who are able-bodied yet refuse to work. (Violates Fourth and Eighth Commandments)

They arrogantly lay claim to state control of our children's physical, emotional, educational, and spiritual well-being. For example, the recent push for outcome-based education is the God-hating social engineer's means of ensuring that children in private or home schools (who are not in the grasp of public education) are taught "positively" about sodomy and lesbianism and fed the baloney about spotted owls and old-growth forests. The attempts of the government to number our children and to demand we immunize our children are simply more ways of government control. They want to give our teen-agers condoms and abortions and recruit them into homosexual circles without parental knowledge or consent. (Violates Fifth Commandment)

They shamelessly promote the murder of innocent pre-born children. They callously tolerate infanticide of the handicapped, and they wring crocodile tears from their handkerchiefs over the lack of "care for the elderly," while praising demonic heroes like Jack Kevorkian as they promote euthanasia. (Violates Sixth Commandment)

They brazenly promote sodomy, lesbianism, fornication in the movies, on the television, and even in schools. New books aimed at first graders have flooded the educational market. Titles such as *Heather Has Two Mommies*, *Daddy's Roommate, Heather Goes to Gay Pride*, etc., are part of the new genre of filth. Many of them openly promote and/or live in adultery. (Violates Seventh Commandment)

When they teach children in public schools about history, they knowingly omit all references to God and Christ, including those that are foundational to our country's beginning. Then they tell us uneducated masses that the founding fathers struggled to keep church and biblical influence out of politics. These are bold-faced lies. (Violates Ninth Commandment)

They promote greed and jealousy with their "soak the rich" tax-scams and public-relations campaigns. "Class warfare" is an unbiblical Marxist tactic that is immorally "redistributing the wealth" and playing on covetousness. (Violates Tenth Commandment)

Do You Know "They"?

By the way, who are "they"?

"They" are the prophets and priests of Clinton's "New Covenant." (The one he promised at the Democratic Convention in 1992.)

"They" are (in random order): the National Organization of Women (NOW); the American Civil Liberties Union (ACLU); the National Education Association (NEA); pagan judges of federal, state, and local benches; the Hollywood elite; Act-Up; Queer Nation; North American Man-Boy Love Association; the majority of newspaper editors and journalists; the majority of television's elite; the American Medical Association (AMA); an army of university deans and professors (educated way beyond their intelligence); the major networks; the Ted Kennedy crowd; the friends of Hillary crowd; the faceless crowd of bureaucrats that have infested our nation; the messianic social-engineers that skulk around in small communities across the nation promoting "tolerance"; Planned Parenthood (curriculum and condoms); the Madonna crowd; the Green Peace crowd; the Al Gore eco-freak crowd; Earth First; People United for the Separation of Church and State; various social service agencies; the Children's Defense League; the child-killers and spineless career politicians who allow these lunatics to terrorize them into promoting iniquity; and the innumerable cadres of bureaucratic, statist thugs who are on a mission to rid the earth of Christian influence and biblical morality. That's who "they" are, just to name a few.

Now I understand that every group and every individual in each group are probably not violating all Ten Commandments at once. Certain eco-freaks might be faithful to their spouses. Truthfully, I know of no pagans who are fully consistent with their moral anarchy. But this paints a very accurate description of where they are headed.

And given their stunning victories in every venue of life, where will we be in ten or twenty or thirty years?

Imagine the Future

Is state-*mandated* education of all children concerning the beauty of homosexuality too far-fetched? How about hiring quotas for the homosexual minority? Or maybe the sex criminals will be successful in their efforts to eliminate pedophile laws. (Then pedophiles can whine about pedophilephobia.)

Is it too far–fetched to believe that preaching the gospel on public streets could be outlawed? After all, it already is illegal in "public" schools and on certain public sidewalks near the sacred child-killing temples. (Besides, you can preach in your church.)

And what about hate crimes? Could speaking against sodomy, speaking against lesbianism, or speaking against any other sacred cow become a crime? On certain university campuses, "hate crimes" regulations aimed at silencing all dissent (in the name of tolerance) have been enacted.

Is it beyond the realm of possibility to envision forced sterilization or forced abortion? What if we have a severe drought and massive food shortages? Isn't it conceivable that all those adults who played "lifeboat" in public school will make the "hard choices" and throw the unwanted "overboard"? (All, of course, for the good of the whole.) Isn't it conceivable that a nation that casually does business with a nation practicing forced sterilization and forced abortion could import their brutal practices as well as their sneakers and toys? After all, Molly Yard has praised China's "birth control" policy and Ted Turner of C.N.N. has suggested a two child per family limit in America with *no outcry* from the public or the press.

In a nation that forbids putting the manger scene on town hall lawns but *pays* for putting a crucifix in a vat of urine, what atrocities will await the church? It's only a matter of time till they declare more and more issues off limits from American pulpits. How many more pastors will be harassed and even imprisoned? As I write, Pete Peters, a pastor in Colorado, has had the church's bank account seized, as well as all of his church's television and radio recording equipment, because he spoke out against a referendum that would have given special rights to sodomites. Charges were brought by the state department. A Colorado judge ruled that because the church had spoken out on a "political" issue, it was a Political Action Committee. And he ordered them to file as one. They refused, saying they were a church. They were fined, and all their assets were seized. The battle is still in earnest.

And what of our children? Is it beyond the realm of imagination that those of us who use corporal punishment on our children will fall prey to those who insist that loving biblical discipline is child abuse? How many families may be broken up by an S. S. agent (Social Services) with an agenda. (It is well documented that many families across the country have already been harassed under such anti-Christian policies.)

And what of the First Amendment rights that Christians take for granted? For example, the so-called "fairness doctrine" could in a moment wipe out 80 percent of Christian radio as a powerful weapon in this cultural civil war. If the "fairness doctrine" is reinstated, a radio station that airs my show would be required to give "equal time" on discussions of issues for the day. Hence, if I host a show concerning sodomy or child-killing, the station would be required to allow some lost rebel to go on the air defending their perversion. As you can guess, a lot of Christian stations would rather turn the lights off than be used to promote a godless agenda. What many stations would do is either play all music or only play shows that talk about "spiritual" things that won't get them in political trouble. (I know, a lot of Christian radio is already like that!)

And what of police powers? Or how about the gun-control nuts who want to destroy our Second Amendment rights? Or what of the eco-freaks who are bearing down on the rights of small business owners? And how many more "Los Angeles riots" will we endure?

Or how about sodomite activists who want to be married and adopt children? What unspeakable perversion today will be extolled tomorrow?

And finally, how long before more and more people snap? How long before enough good people say "enough!"? We sat and watched the "fall of communism" and the break-up of nations from the comfort of our armchairs. Most Christians believe it was the judgment of God on wicked governments and the blessing of God poured out on His people in those countries. Could we live to see the break-up of America? Could God judge our pagan government and bless His people with freedom? Could the spirit of the founders again find lodging in the hearts of grief-stricken, freedom-loving Americans? Then what? God only knows. In the meantime, remember friend, you are not immune. The most ardent escapist is not safe. The most studied separatist will not be immune from their plans. We cannot hide our heads in the sand and pretend the danger will go away, the wickedness will simply subside. That kind of thinking for the past generation has helped deliver us into the jaws of Hell.

Are you seeing the need to stand and be counted? To fight for righteousness? If you do, God will bless you as you take a stand for Him. However, your courage and activity will not go unnoticed. We have some powerful enemies. As the saying goes, "No good deed goes unpunished."

As you stand—especially as your church takes a stand—you may find you are in for an unwanted relationship with the Internal Revenue Service.

And, as a measure against the Confessing Church, pastors were required to obtain advance approval for the objects of their collections in case the money might be used to support activities regarded as illegal by the State.[1]

The National Socialist State has neither closed a church nor prevented a church service, still less tried to influence the form of any church liturgy. It has not sought to alter the teaching of the creeds of any denomination. In the National Socialist State, everyone can be saved in his own fashion.

The National Socialist State will ruthlessly bring to their senses any priests, who, instead of serving God, think it their mission to vilify our present Reich, its institutions, or its leaders. The destruction of this State will not be tolerated from anyone . . . . We will protect the German priest who is the servant of God, we will wipe out the priest who is a political enemy of the German Reich.[2]

Adolf Hitler

Fourteen

BATTLING THE INTERNAL REVENUE SERVICE

(Spitting Out the Government's Bit and Bridle)

When the Church at Pierce Creek took out the full-page advertisement in *U.S.A. Today* and then the *Washington Times* saying "Christian Beware: Do not put the economy ahead of the ten commandments," we were excited. Reverend Little was taking a courageous and controversial stand, yet we were confident that we were on solid biblical ground, prophesying the Word of God to the church and the nation.

Furthermore, we were confident we were on firm constitutional ground. Our warning was clearly aimed to Christians, based on the Word of God, and the free exercise of our religion—including such a prophetic witness—could not be abridged. We were discussing Christian issues, issues clearly dealt with in the Bible.

They contacted us and basically had the gall to say that child-killing, sodomy, and condom pushing to our children were *political*, not Christian issues. The Internal Revenue Service arrogated to the government and the political realm (and to themselves) "issues" relating to three of the Ten Commandments (don't kill; don't com-

mit adultery; honor your mother and father). In a ploy
reminiscent of the Nazis in the mid-1930s, an entire realm
of debate that was intrinsically spiritual by government
decree became instantly political, and hence off limits to
the church.

My pastor, Reverend Daniel J. Little, never flinched,
never wavered, never looked back. When they requested
a list of our donors, he politely refused. When they posed
to him a list of intrusive questions, he answered with
lengthy passages of the Bible showing that the people of
God have a duty to be watchmen on the wall warning the
nation against walking in a path of wickedness. Reverend
Little understood that the crux of our debate with the
Internal Revenue Service was simply: Who is Lord of the
church—Christ or Caesar? Who will tell the church what
to say—Christ or Caesar?

After a few pointed correspondences by phone and
letter, Reverend Little reached for the core of the argument and sent this letter to the Internal Revenue Service:

Dear Sir:

I am in receipt of your letter of February 11, 1993
wherein you have made an informal request to see
certain records of The Church at Pierce Creek.

Our quarterly board meeting is planned for the first
Monday of April, 1993. In order to help me present
this to my church board, I need to know where it is
that we have gone wrong.

What your letters convey to me is this: that once a
church is recognized as being tax exempt, that that
church can no longer use its funds to warn other
Christians of perceived dangers if those dangers are
in some way connected to anything political, and that
this prohibition is universal in its scope; it may not
warn by the spoken word from the pulpit or over the
public airways, or by means of the written word—
letters or media such as magazines or newspapers.
**Am I correct in my perception of what you are say-
ing to us?**

I am asking for this clarification for a very important reason, in that at present I am caught between a desire and a fear. On the one hand I desire to urge the board to cooperate with you so that you may see for yourself the upright nature of this local church, on the other hand, I fear—deeply fear that because we are tax exempt, the IRS holds authority and final say in what the church says and does. Are my fears founded in fact?

Stated more specifically my question is this: because the IRS recognizes us as being tax exempt, can the IRS now say to our church, **"You cannot communicate warnings to the church at large about the dangers of abandoning the established moral law of the Holy Bible"?** Are you saying that, **Because the abandonment of these Biblically established moral laws is now established as political policy that these moral issues have now been lifted out of the church's domain?** I ask for this clarification for the simple reason that I must present this matter to my board with absolute clarity in order that they might give an informed answer to your requests.

As for myself, I am in a dilemma. It seems that we have unwittingly given you power to govern the church in the matter of our message in that **if at any time moral issues become carefully couched in the language of political policy that the IRS is set to say that the tax exempt church no longer has a right to address those issues. Isn't that giving over to the State what actually belongs to the church? And what happens if all moral law becomes political?**

It was Justices Black and Douglas who co-wrote a 1958 Supreme Court majority opinion which, in part read:

"There is no power in Government to make one bend his religious scruples to the requirements of a tax law."

Our religious scruples are such that we must warn any who will listen of the dangers of abandoning the moral law of the Holy Bible for any reason—be it political policy or personal preference. In the courtroom debate over this same case Justice Black asked the prosecuting attorney;

"Doesn't this give the legislature the right to measure doctrine?"

A later scholarly review of this case concluded:

"If the State can discriminate in regard to taxes among religious groups on the basis of what they are willing to declare as their views in an area where religion and politics meet the State is itself declaring what is and what is not patriotic religious orthodoxy, and freedom of **conscience has ceased to exist."**

Did our warning to the church break the law? If so how? And how will examining our finances help you to know whether our warning broke the law? **Are we being examined because politics has recently crossed the moral boundaries which have been so clearly defined in the Holy Scriptures for four millennia?**

In our national history we have these words from the House Judiciary Committee Report March 3, 1854. They were written in response to a request that all reference to religion be removed from government. After a year long investigation, the committee concluded:

"Had the people, during the Revolution, had any suspicion of any attempt to war against Christianity, the Revolution would have been strangled in the cradle. At the time of the adoption of the Constitution and the Amendments, the universal sentiment was that Christianity should be encouraged, not any one sect. In this age there can be no substitute for Christianity. That was the religion of the founders of the republic, and they expected it to remain the religion of their descendants. The great vital and conservative element in our system is the doctrines and divine truths of the gospel of Jesus Christ."

And there are these words found in Andrew Jackson's farewell address:

"There is, perhaps, no one of the powers conferred on the federal government so liable to abuse as the taxing power."

We understand that the IRS wields considerable temporal power, and therefore, assure you that we are operating well within the governing boundaries of Holy Scriptures, that we are in perfect harmony with the history of the Christian church at large and particularly in this nation, and that we are ready to cooperate to the fullest extent possible as you make our offense clear to us. **I must humbly admit to you that I do not understand how our warning to the church would put us at odds with tax law.**

Hopefully your reply will come before our board meeting. If, however, your answer should come after we have held our quarterly meeting, we will hold a special session where I will present your request to them to the best of my ability.

Sincerely and with respect,
Rev. Daniel J. Little

We have yet to receive an answer.

Soon after this letter, *Christianity Today* asked Reverend Little to write a guest column for their magazine. His thoughtful warning to the church bears repeating:

SPEAKING OUT

Don't Let the IRS Rule the Church

Just before last year's presidential election, my church bought full page ads in *USA Today* and the *Washington Times*. In them we warned Christians of what we thought were the dangers of voting for a presidential candidate who supports homosexual rights, lifting regulations on abortion, and distributing condoms in public schools.

Not long afterward, we heard from the Internal Revenue Service. These matters are *political*, the IRS explained, and the church must be silent on them. Speaking out on them violates IRS code on tax-exempt organizations.

The IRS proceeded to ask us for a mountain of information, including the names and addresses of financial supporters, so it could determine if a "church inquiry" was called for. While in good conscience we could not respond to all of their requests, we did supply several pages of Bible-based explanations of the church's identity and role. At press time, our response was still under review.

When CHRISTIANITY TODAY covered the incident (Dec. 14, 1992, p. 64) it used the headline "Church Tests Political Limits." The magazine should have called the story "Government Tests Limits of the Church."

Has tax exemption become a means for government to control the church? Evidently the government thinks so. And by their meticulous compliance, many pastors, church boards, and Christian leaders seem to support that position.

Some of God's watchmen bear powerful oracles of warning that should be delivered clearly and unapologetically. Yet, just as Judah relied on the "broken reed" of Egypt's protection (Isa. 36:6), those watchmen hold back for fear of losing tax-exempt status.

Too often, reproving the works of darkness or warning the saints is no longer a matter of "What saith the Scriptures," but "What said the IRS." Too many churches view tax exemption as a tenuously held privilege—a monthly lease paid for by surrendering the right to speak on the issues of the day.

This has not always been the case. Our Founders understood the church to be separate from government jurisdiction—not tax exempt, but tax *immune.* To tax was to exercise civil control in church affairs.

But lately, government has been acting as though it has a *right* to tax the church—and is doing the church a favor by leaving tax dollars in the church larder. This, in their view, amounts to subsidizing the church.

In return for this generous subsidy, the church and its watchmen are expected to bow obsequiously before government censors.

But this must not continue. We churches that hold to moral absolutes will find ourselves more and more out of step with the culture around us. We exist on the foundation of eternal, immutable rules. And one facet of our calling is to try all things by God's Word and expose the works of darkness.

We cannot allow tax exemption to become the bit by which government controls the church's mouth in that prophetic role.

We must begin by refusing to act upon a nonexistent agreement. No church that cares for the lordship of Christ ever understood or agreed that tax exemption means being government registered and controlled.

We do not need permission to speak on moral matters or to publish ads that warn other Christians about what we believe are the works of darkness. We may do this freely, on local or national levels, and we may do it without fear of the government. Also, if they so choose, people may freely give of their finances to support the church in this task.

But suppose the worst. Suppose we are forced to surrender our tax-exempt status. The loss could become a gain. We could, as it were, cast down the broken reed that splinters in our hand and embrace anew the lordship of Christ and his Word. And his words, Isaiah reminds us, put teeth into the mouth of worms—teeth that even worms can use to crush mountains and make hills into chaff.

As you can see, the specter that hangs over all 501(C) (3) churches and ministries is horrifying. The government is already well on their way to telling us what are acceptable "spiritual discussions" and what they deem inappropriate political discussions. (I wonder why none of the churches where Jesse Jackson has campaigned have been harassed.)

Tragically, many churches and ministries have already made a conscious decision to obey the dictates of the Internal Revenue Service, rather than the dictates of God's Word. The net effect of this will be calamitous. Consider what may await us.

1. We will be under constant threat of harassing investigations if we broach spiritual issues that have become (or at any minute may become) "political."

2. Many churches, pastors, ministries, etc. will abandon their biblical duty to be watchmen on the walls and will scrupulously avoid anything that would endanger their precious tax-exempt status. They will have bowed the knee to the golden calf and said, "These are your gods, O Israel, who brought you out of Egypt" (Exod. 32:4c).

3. A small number (my guess) will tell the Internal Revenue Service and the federal government, "You have neither part nor lot with us in this matter" (Acts 8:21), the church of God is not under your authority, but Christ's. Our tax-exempt status be damned if it keeps us from declaring the whole counsel of God.

4. A clear (and tragic) division will occur in the church between the state-sanctioned churches and the "Confessing Church" or the Resistance which cleaves to the whole Word of God and the whole duty of the church.

5. Ichabod ("no more glory") will be written over the doors of those churches/ministries that sell out for a few shekels of silver, and they will slowly wither and die. But tragically in the meantime, they will boast of their yet secure "tax-deductible donation" status to their donors, who may be poisoned by that spirit that helped the ministry retain its tax-exempt status. Worse yet, those supporters may be effectively castrated from any sense of duty to fight in the great battles of our day. This will help expedite the moral collapse of our culture.

And then what? Who knows. Such "reasoned" compromise between Christian churches and the Nazi state helped pave the way for the death of millions and the oppression of an entire continent and parts of three others.

What nightmares lie ahead of us if our Christian leaders continue trying to curry the favor of those bent on silencing and destroying them?

Our warnings about Clinton were none too strong. After taking office, he moved with speed in the shedding of innocent blood and the promotion of sodomy; it was a blitzkrieg of wickedness that surprised many of his fellow God-haters.

His attorney general, Janet Reno, made her "top priority" the persecution and crushing of discordant pro-lifers. Notice that her first words did not lash out at drug lords, or mafia bosses; she didn't decry gang-warfare or car-jackings, or even mail and credit card fraud. No, she lashed out at Christians and set her unjust sights squarely on pro-life activists. People truly do govern in accordance with their ethical allegiances. For her, preserving child-killing is evidently more important than stopping cocaine sales.

Our church ran the full-page advertisement warning Christians against putting money ahead of the Ten Commandments; over one hundred sixty similar advertisements ran across the nation; hundreds of thousands of flyers were handed out clearly explaining why "To vote for Clinton was to sin against God!" And yet, millions of Christians deserted biblical morality in search of gold.

Now that our nation is feeling the impact of this folly, as it probably will for years and years to come, and now that pro-lifers will be pursued and persecuted with frightening vigor, I want to give a heartfelt "thanks" to all my brothers and sisters in Christ who put their money ahead of the Law of God, the lives of babies, and the security of our military. Thanks for putting your selfish greed ahead of the freedom and welfare of your pro-life brethren. Thanks for selling us all out. Thanks.

The altar is open for you to repent.

And now, as the church is being "trampled under foot of men" (as Jesus promised we would be if we were not faithful), history will remember your betrayal in a special way, because you helped expedite the judgment of God on the church and the nation. Moreover, you have left a legacy of confusion and compromise to your children and grandchildren. Let's hope future generations learn *not* to follow this example. God forgive us all.

And let's pray that the church does not continue to

sell its birthright for some 501(C)(3) pottage. God help us to spit the government's bit out of our mouths and tear the bridle off our heads. We must no longer agree to have the government buy our silence.

And so, is all lost? Have we sold out with no hope of redemption? Is the oppressive, frightening, bloody scenario I painted earlier a forgone conclusion, an inescapable destiny because of our folly? Absolutely not—if we in the church once again live, move, and speak as the church.

If the church acknowledges her guilt of silence and cowardice that has led to the collapse of our culture; if we will obey and proclaim the whole counsel of God, we can become the core of righteous resistance. God can restore us and grant us the vision and the strategy to systematically take back the power bases of our culture. America can once again be what the pilgrims and the founders sought after—a city on a hill, an example to the world, a covenant, Christian nation.

We preferred to keep quiet. We are most certainly not without guilt; and I ask myself over and over again what would have happened if 14,000 evangelical ministers and the Evangelical communities, all over Germany, had defended the truth with their very lives in the year 1933 or 1934, when there must have been a possibility? If we had said then that it is not just for Herman Goering simply to throw 100,000 communists into concentration camps to perish?

I can imagine that 30 to 40 thousand Evangelical Christians would have been shortened by a head, but I can also imagine that we would have thus saved 30-40 millions of lives, for this is the price that we now have to pay.[1]

Martin Niemöller

We are in danger of losing God's grace through our own disloyalty. Therefore we must ask our brethren to examine their hearts to see if they are ready for the future struggle. . . . In recent months we have been waiting for the decisive success of our Church administration and for the official recognition by the State of the Confessing Church. But we have only received one disappointment after another. Many of us are therefore tired and despondent. But we must recognize that it is our faithlessness which has caused us to put our trust in men rather than in God.[2]

Martin Niemöller

The world is at this moment passing through one of those terrible periods of convulsion when the souls of men and of nations are tried as by fire. Woe to the man or to the nation that at such a time stands as once Laodicea stood; as the people of ancient Meroz stood, when they dared not come to the help of the Lord against the mighty. In such a crisis the moral weakling is the enemy of the right, the enemy of life, liberty, and the pursuit of happiness.[3]

Theodore Roosevelt

Fifteen

WHAT MUST WE DO TO BE SAVED?
(Repentance, Resistance, Reformation)

Don't give up the ship! Don't give up the ship! Before you feel like quitting because the challenge is too great, the chance of victory too slim, consider this:

Most of the major power bases in America and in Western civilization have *distinctly Christian roots*. For example, where did hospitals come from? The church. Where did most children learn to read and write? The church. Who founded America's first universities (Harvard, Yale, Princeton)? Christians. What was printed from the first printing press? A Bible. What theme dominated the arts for centuries? Christianity. What do men swear on in a court of law? A Bible.

Where does the concept of hierarchical, representative government come from? The Bible. Most of the founders of this nation were Trinitarian Christians or Deists who believed the Bible was the foundation of culture, law, and order.

This is our heritage! Our forefathers developed most of what we call "civilization." The challenge before us is to restore these citadels of power to their original biblical foundations.

Tragically, what the church founded to be bastions of mercy and justice have become the haunts of jackals, dark towers of death, misery and cruelty. But even as God restored ancient Israel after the Babylonian captivity, and He promised that the glory of the "latter house" would be greater than the first (see Hag. 2:9), so America's future could be one of greater justice, greater righteousness, and greater God-centered life than our origins.

So don't despair! You may be tempted to say, "I'm just going to batten down the hatch and try to ride out the storm with my family and property intact. I'm going to be a survivalist."

In one way, that's not such a bad plan. Certainly, that must be a critical part of our plan.

Times of Crisis Produce New Leaders

However, we don't want to be like the Christians of Eastern Europe who survived the Nazi nightmare only to wake up in the icy grasp of Stalinist communism.

When America's current moral decay results in a cataclysmic cultural collapse—which it certainly will—we don't want to be buried beneath the rubble. And we don't want iron-fisted tyrants "rebuilding" America. Remember, the economic chaos of Germany in the late 1920s and early 1930s was a precursor to Adolf Hitler. He could never have amassed so much power so quickly had Germany not been in desperate straits.

While the circumstances that led to Germany's vulnerability to tyrants will probably not be duplicated in America, certainly the desperation of individuals, families, and entire communities could pave the way for strong-armed tyrants who promise to restore order and stability. We *cannot* let this happen.

With the help of God, and the Bible as our guidebook and blueprint, we must do our best to insure that God-fearing men and women are leading America out of the coming darkness, that Ten Commandment-oriented reformers are serving the nation as statesmen. We need a new wave of Wilberforces, Witherspoons, John Adamses, George Washingtons, Patrick Henrys, Deborahs, and men and women of their caliber and vision to restore liberty and righteousness in the land.

So how do we get from here to there? How do we prepare for leadership on the other side of the collapse?

Answer: Repentance, Resistance, Reformation.

God Forgive Us

The first thing we need to do is repent. We need to repent of the selfishness, the escapism, the self-preservation, the if-it-doesn't-affect-me-and-mine attitude that has helped destroy America. We Christians must accept the fact that America could never have decayed so rapidly and so severely without the participation (or cultural lack thereof) of the church. We are the light of the world. If darkness is prevailing, it is because our light is under a bushel. We are the salt of the world. If righteousness is not being preserved, then we are worthless salt.

Like the prophet Daniel in Daniel 9, we must plead with God for mercy and forgiveness for our sins and the sins of our fathers and contemporaries. I have sinned, and *we* have sinned. Even if all of "we" don't see our sin, or even if you and I didn't *personally* do every evil deed (or fail to do every good deed) that has resulted in this mess, we must repent as a people.

We have been unfaithful to the covenant; *we* have not unashamedly held up God's Word to our nation; *we* have wilted under fire from the enemies' camp; *we* have surrendered our post as watchmen for a tax-exempt mess of pottage; *we* have traded the glory of God's look for the similitude of an ox—conservative humanism; *we* have loved our reputation more than the cross of Christ; *we* have sinned grievously before heaven.

And what of our children? We have entertained them but not discipled them. Our children know the Saturday morning cartoons but not the Ten Commandments and the Apostles' Creed. We have sinned against our children by not training them and leading them by example into a Christ-centered, sacrificial life. Is it any wonder that the church has lost so many of her children to the world when they have become adults? They have seldom witnessed in us a Christianity worth living, fighting, and dying for.

Harvest Is Great

When we truly repent of self-centered separatist Christianity, we will see true revival—like the revivals we read about: a revival that results in the lost being converted. I'm convinced when we truly live and preach Christ, we can see a great ingathering of souls—not to become pew-potatoes, but to become ambassadors and warriors for Christ.

Many of the mockers will become converts; many of our enemies will become our brethren and fellow servants of God.

As we repent—and fearlessly preach the gospel—we have no idea how many new converts may come into the kingdom. During the great "revivals" and "ingatherings" in America and Europe during the 1700s and 1800s, many cities that had been filled with debauchery and drunkenness became citadels of righteousness and justice as multitudes came to Christ.

Thought-Out Prayers

I heartily encourage you to have prepared prayers of repentance that you can pray alone and in groups. Cry out to God that He will forgive us for squandering the freedoms our forefathers fought and died for; beg His forgiveness for spending our children's future welfare and freedom on our current comfort and ease. Confess our sins of compromise and retreat before our enemies. Ask God's forgiveness for allowing the wicked to dominate the day, for abandoning the centers of power that Jesus has called us to serve in.

Bearing Fruits of Repentance

As you hopefully know, true repentance involves confession *and action.* Having asked God's forgiveness for the evil deeds we have done, we must desist from wickedness "and sin no more" (John 8:11b).

Likewise, "to one who knows the right thing to do, and does not do it, to him it is sin" (James 4:17). If we have failed to do good, we must repent of our sin of omission and show our repentance by doing the works of God. If we have failed to speak God's Word, we must declare it. If we have failed to stand publicly on the Ten Commandments, we must begin doing so. If we have failed to fight in our communities for what is right—whether teaching chastity in the schools or closing the porno shop—we must fight. If we have neglected the children and mothers scheduled to go under the abortionist's knife, we must come to their aid.

If we have neglected the state, if we have not voted, or not aided in the election of godly people to various offices, it's time to enter the fray. The Bible says, "When the righteous are in authority, the people rejoice: but when the wicked beareth rule, the people mourn" (Prov. 29:2). We are now mourning because wicked men rule.

Our repentance must not be esoteric, solely spiritual, or solely be the confession of sin; our repentance must bear *practical, tangible* fruit. As the Scripture says, "Bring forth fruit in keeping with your repentance" (Matt. 3:8). Let me say it this way: If your heart has been convicted, if you acknowledge that you have sinned by commission or omission and yet your life is unchanged, then you have not truly repented.

One critical fruit of our repentance is that we abandon escapism. Whether you have been waylaid by date-setting rapture fever, whether you are the victim of a separatist Christianity mentality, or whether you are simply trying to protect your own backside, stop looking for a quick, cheap means of escape. "The battle is the Lord's" (1 Sam. 17:47b), but we are called to the battle. "He teaches my hands to war" (Ps. 18:34). He has not called us to sit on the sideline and be observers or cheerleaders in the great conflicts of our day. He has called us to be warriors for truth.

The Resistance

The Scripture declares, "Those who forsake the law praise the wicked, but those who keep the law resist them" (Prov. 28:4). Yes, the neo-pagans have successfully engineered a coup d'état due largely to our selfish drunkenness. But now that we are sober, we must fight to displace them, school by school, university by university, newspaper by newspaper, judgeship by judgeship, congressman by congressman.

Read the book of Judges, and you will see a simple scenario over and over. The people of God enter into idolatry. God then chastens them by handing them over to wicked enemies to be ruled over and oppressed (see Psalm 106:34-42). When the people of God repent of their idolatry, they are not suddenly freed of their oppressors and restored to a place of authority. *They have to displace their oppressors.* No magic wand, no quick prayer, but real confrontation and conflict, real courage and sacrifice, real blood, sweat, and tears are needed to restore liberty.

It will be the same here. Victory will not be quick, easy, or cheap. It will be timely, difficult, and costly. But it will be a lot more costly if we don't resist. The thought of a one- or two-hundred-year dark ages should be sufficient to motivate us to stand.

Practical Suggestions of Resistance

And so, what should you do in the resistance? Here are some suggested activities that virtually any Christian can be involved in.

If you hear of a brother or sister who is being harassed in any manner, shape, or form by a bureaucrat, a school superintendent, a police department, a judge, etc., rise to their defense. Call and write the government official, demanding they back off. Picket their place of work or the neighborhood in which they live. Send them a clear message: "If you mess with a few of us, you're going to deal with a lot of us."

If you learn of a proposed curriculum in your public school district that disturbs you with its anti-Godly principles (even though your kids are in private or home school), attend public meetings or apply public and private pressure to keep the curriculum out. If it's already in, get it out.

When you hear of some godless law or statute being enacted in the federal government, in your state, in your county, or in your city—whether it's for special sodomite "rights," or to make abortion mill pickets illegal, or to change a zoning law to make room for a strip joint—oppose the legislation. Visit the legislators involved, demanding they stand against godless legislation. Threaten them with "early retirement" if they cave in to the wicked. Speak to your friends in church to mobilize greater numbers to speak out. Call in to radio talk shows. Organize a public protest. Get a half dozen people, make some signs, call the press and the media, and away you go. Utilize the media as a means of prophesying to your community.

If you learn that a New Ager or a sodomite or a baby-killer or a condom pusher is going to address the students in a school, insist that the invitation be withdrawn. If need be, create an unpleasant fuss with a few outraged moms and dads. If that fails, insist that someone be allowed to give an "opposing view."

If you learn that your local television station is planning to run a propaganda piece for enemies of the gospel, demand that the show be cancelled, or insist on equal time.

Make it your blueprint: Stand against wickedness. When the wicked are promoting rebellion against God's Word, when they are seeking to pollute the minds of youth—whether in blatant sexual sins, or through statist messianic welfarism, resist them.

Tax—Theft

One key area Christians must resist in now (but unfortunately we have been woefully silent in) is the con-
tinual government theft of our substance and wealth. God
only requires 10 percent of our substance, yet our federal
government requires millions of us to pay 15, 27, even 33
percent, plus state, local, land, school, and sales tax—
before we even get into hidden fees, fuel taxes, licenses,
etc. It is arguable that for the state to take more than God
is immoral, that the state is arrogating to itself a near
divine call for sacrifice and obedience. Yes, we must ren-
der to Caesar what is Caesar's, but does Caesar have the
right to endlessly plunder? We must be firm in our resistance to the messianic-statist-socialist plundering of our
wealth and our children's inheritance.

If this line of reasoning catches you off guard, I ask
you this question: Would the government have the right
to take 90 percent of our money for taxes? If we gave God
His 10 percent, we would have nothing left! (see 1 Samuel
8:10-18; the government taking 10 percent was considered horrifying!)

Future Credibility Earned Today

One key role of resistance in this hour is that of prophetic warning: We must oppose the prophets of Baal—
the social elite who think they can build a better society
than the one laid out in the Scriptures.

We must continue to warn the citizenry at large of the
consequences that await us for rejecting God and His
Word: mayhem and upheaval (read Deuteronomy 28).
We must clearly define the calamities that await the individual, the family, the community, and our nation because we have rebelled against God's Word.

Furthermore, we must offer the cures to current and
future crises *now*. We must herald the biblical solutions
today, though they are already unpopular.

The Churchill Challenge

As you might guess, such advice won't always be welcome right now, but this must not dissuade nor discourage us. Let us look to Winston Churchill for encouragement. Throughout the 1930s Churchill warned Parliament and all England of the growing Nazi menace. He declared England would be deluged by a "rain of fire and steel."

Churchill was bold. He was clear. He had his facts straight. He had read *Mein Kampf.* He was blaming British leaders for putting all Britain in danger and challenging them to act speedily to undo the damage their cowardice and folly had done. Yet he was mocked and vilified. The press called him a fearmonger and a warmonger. He was ridiculed by fellow members of Parliament. *But he was right.* And when all hell broke loose in Europe, the nation looked to Winston Churchill for leadership and vision, because he had told them the truth. Churchill earned credibility because he unflinchingly told them what was true even when it was unpopular.

We must do the same. We must give warning and solutions now, even though they are unpopular or even ridiculed and rejected. When calamity fully comes, we want to be able to say, "We warned you. We told you this would happen. We have reaped the fruit of forsaking God. This is what we must do to rebuild."

Blame Is Critical

We want the pagans and God-haters and egalitarian Socialist planners to bear the blame for leading our country into a wasteland. (We do not want to be a scapegoat for the pagans when America's collapse comes.) We want their heathen, hedonistic philosophy to bear the blame for the AIDS plague. We want their messianic-state-socialist programs to bear the blame for America's economic bankruptcy. We want their pagan belief structure to bear the blame for America's moral bankruptcy. We want the pagan's signature on America's burned churches.

Then we will be in a position of strength to lead the country out of moral and social chaos. Like Churchill, we will have the stature in the culture and the respect of our fellow citizens to lead the way out of chaos.

Otherwise—if we don't point out the dangers and solutions now—we may find ourselves as the scapegoat for the pagans. As in Rome, when America burns, the Neros of our day will blame the Christians. We can already see the first fruits of this in art and education. Christianity and Christians are vilified as the enemy. We are blamed for intolerance, the spread of AIDS, disunity in America, brainwashing our children, etc.

We cannot be silent now. We must resist on all fronts at all costs.

Reformation

As you can see, the role of resistance is primarily confrontational and is often defensive as well as offensive (in more than one way!). But while this is critical, it is not the whole realm of duty for Christians. We must not simply be reactionaries, ever responding to the maneuvers of our enemies.

If we are going to reclaim and rebuild the power bases of this culture, we must have a clearly defined vision of what we plan to achieve by God's strength and according to His Word.

What Exactly Will We Do?

What will a Christian America look like? What will education, medicine, the arts, the entertainment industry, newspapers, the judiciary, and legislatures look like when they are built on the foundation of the Ten Commandments? What will constitute a crime? How will criminals be punished? How will banking be different—will we continue with fractional banking and fiat money, both of which are inherently fraudulent, or will our reforms reach to our monetary systems? What will poverty relief and care of widows look like?

If we are going to succeed in reforming our nation—or any successor nations should the United States break up—*we must have vision,* for without vision we dwell carelessly, we cast off restraint, we perish (Prov. 29:18).

You would do well to slowly think through, or at least begin to imagine, what a reformed America will look and behave like. It's easy to say, "No more abortion! No special rights for sodomites! No tax-funded blasphemy!" Those arenas are critical—and obvious—but the Word of God addresses much more than that. The collapse of our country is comprehensive; our vision for reformation must likewise be comprehensive.

Some arenas will take a generation to reform; others could be revitalized in a few years. For example, virtually every political institution could have new statesmen in six years. However, universities with tenured professors (who still teach Marxist communism) and judgeships with lifetime appointments will obviously take more time. We must focus on both.

Vision Begets Strategy

From vision, strategy naturally flows. Strategies will be different, uniquely crafted to different situations. If you are a vision-driven man or woman, you will create (or stumble) on a strategy to accomplish your vision. As I said earlier, if you were an Israelite in ancient Israel, and your vision was to fight Philistines, you might have done it with a sword; you might have used a spear; you may have used a sling and a stone; or you might even have employed the jawbone of an ass. The tools are secondary to accomplishing the vision.

Likewise, we must have a vision for reforming this culture and develop the tools and strategy for rebuilding the waste places.

Some broad vision concepts of reformation follow.

Our Children

Our most precious resource is our children. Our only eternal possession besides our own soul is our children. It has become glaringly apparent to me that while we have begun this battle for America's soul, our children will have to finish it. That means we need a long-range vision which includes godly offspring.

We need first to adhere to the Bible's view of children—they are a blessing, a reward from God, arrows in the hands of a mighty warrior; blessed is the man whose quiver is full of them (see Ps. 127). I'm convinced the Protestant community needs to return to its pre-1900 stand on birth control for Christian couples. It's a tragedy that the church has adopted the "less is more" view of Planned Parenthood concerning our children. "Children are a burden; I only want two; I'm going to get sterilized." Let me use a biblical allusion. The Bible says children are the arrows in our quiver for battle. Who would *deliberately* plunge into a life and death struggle with only one or two arrows!

The next step, if at all humanly possible (and in 90 percent of the cases it is), is to get our children out of the humanistic, brainwashing institution called "public education." Frankly, it is a mixture of insanity and irresponsibility to turn our children over to our adversaries and their curriculum in a God-less education system (i.e., a system that teaches history and science without God).

Lest someone use the argument, "My children are missionaries," let me respond succinctly: Nowhere in the Bible are children sent as missionaries. Other parents vainly argue, "They've got to get used to the real world." However, we husbands would never let our wives work in an office where they were grabbed, propositioned, belittled, and offered drugs on a regular basis. So why would we put our daughters and sons through such a gauntlet of degradation and intimidation, especially since they are in the more vulnerable formative years? And what could be any more real than the world we envision with Christ as King and His Word as Law? Anything else is pure fantasy.

By the way . . . both my parents are public school teachers! There are some fine Christian teachers in public education. I am fully in support of Christian teachers being missionaries in public schools, living and testifying Christ. However, we should keep our children out and ultimately seek to sink the current public education fiasco and replace it with voucher, parent choice education. One could even go one step further and question the validity of state-mandated education. (Before state-mandated education, we had a higher literacy rate. Then the burden to provide education fell squarely where it should have— on the parents!) In the meantime, we need to give our children a God-centered education, day in and day out. Moreover on a "vision" level, we need to teach them that they are different, set apart unto God for His purposes and glory, that they must serve and lead the next generation when they grow up.

Don't worry, I'm not talking about raising our children in a sterile, stuffy atmosphere, void of the fun of childhood. Anyone who knows me can attest that I am ever playing and romping with my children, wrestling in the yard, playing kick ball or hide-and-seek, or reading to them. Our children should love life and should be filled with happy, secure memories.

However, along with love and joy, our children must also learn through our words and our example that we are on a sacred mission from King Jesus to reach this world for Him and to extend the dominion of this kingdom. We are Christians: We love the unlovely, we aid the downtrodden, we fight for justice, we rebuke the oppressors, we rescue the perishing, all for the love of God and man.

The Brightest and the Best

We must carefully study our children, their gifts, their personality traits, their strengths and weaknesses, and then nurture a vision of them excelling in the area of their gifts. More specifically, we need to raise up a generation of leaders. We must deliberately raise up first-class artists and authors, judges and statesmen, doctors and deans of universities, editors of newspapers and journalists for magazines. If you have a child who is always trying to pursue the guilty, maybe he or she is a future prosecutor! If he or she is always journalizing experiences or writing short stories, you may have a budding author on your hands, or a future editor.

Tragically, for two generations much of the church has taken its brightest and best and told them, "Be a pastor! Be a missionary!" That is fine, but for some of them we should have said, "Be a banker! Be a congressman! Be a publisher! Be a rancher! Be a mayor! Be a principal!"

If we expect our children to be sacrificial and courageous, we must exemplify kindness and show a stout heart in adversity. If we want our children to blaze new trails, they have to see us faithfully leading and struggling in the field of battle in which God has posted us. If we expect our children to excel, they cannot see us as addicted to mediocrity. One more quick thought—the current public education fiasco is going to leave a dearth of skilled writers. Do your best to make sure your children read well and extensively, and that they develop to the fullest their skills as a writer. It may be very useful in many vocations.

Pick Your Power Base

Which "power base" grabs your attention? Where does injustice and inequity trouble you the most? Which battlefield in our cultural civil war consumes your thoughts? "If I could only do such and so . . ." Is it the universities? Hospitals and medicine? Politics? Education? The law? How about the arts? Maybe it's film-making. Maybe it's your local tax burden, or perhaps poverty relief.

Chances are, where your thoughts run, God is calling you. I vividly recall when I thought I was called to be a missionary to Central America. I would often pray, "Oh God. Could I just stay back here long enough to fight abortion and then I'll go fulfill my real call?" In those days, because of my "I'm just called to preach the gospel" theology, saving children was a distraction, not a calling.

Maybe you're the same way. You work at a job, but your thoughts are always revolving around reforming education. Or you own your own business, but your heart wishes you were a state representative or a congressman. Perhaps you are a Sunday School superintendent, but you watch your local district attorney like a hawk, and you wish you were an attorney. Maybe you have an intense desire to start your own business.

Well, maybe it's time you stepped out on the water. You've only got one life. Don't waste it.

Know Your Power Base

Get the vision and strategy for reforming the power base, the institution that you feel pulled toward. Go through the tedious, disciplined work of learning everything you can about that field. When did it originate? Who were the key founders? When did it go astray? Who led it astray? Who are the key players now? What must be done to displace those players, or consign them to a less harmful sphere? How far can you go in confronting, exposing, infiltrating, or reforming that arena?

These are some of the questions you must ask. And you must be prepared to spend months, years, maybe decades in a certain battle. Consider William Wilberforce, the great British abolitionist. He labored for *over sixty years* before he finally saw slavery abolished from the British realm. He had many heartaches, many defeats along the way, but he never lost heart, and never lost sight of his goal. The whole world was altered by this man's passion and patience. There was *no quick fix*.

Do you want to be a judge? First go to law school. A

congressman? Then win a city or county office first. Do you want to be an editor of a newspaper, or the owner of one? First be a topflight journalist and a successful small businessman. Do you want to be on a local school board? First attend several meetings, find out who the allies are, who the enemies are, and what the key issues in your district are (besides condom distribution or a Planned Parenthood curriculum). Find out when school board elections are held, and what you have to do to get your name on the ballot. Then do it!

To be a reformer, you must know your field extensively. That requires dedication, time, commitment, and perhaps most importantly, a sense of divine duty—a commission.

Remember, you may never fully achieve your goal. You may pave the way for others. You may look like a radical, while the next guy who comes along believes just as you do and is considered a moderate—because you were the trailblazer, the John the Baptist, the Joseph, the Nehemiah, the radical Ezra type. Not to worry. The goal is to obey and glorify God for the extension of His kingdom. If He uses our toil as the mat upon which the victors enter, glory to His Name! Thank God for the privilege of having been used by Him to prepare the way.

Conclusion

It's hard for me to finish a book like this. I know I've shared some out-of-step, revolutionary thoughts (for a lot of American Christians). My hope is that you will have an inner revelation and vision on what it means to be a Christian and a revolution of thought and deed concerning your duties in this world. Finally, I pray you see what is at stake for future generations if we fail to stand now, while we still can.

Those saints who have gone before us have left us a legacy of courage and sacrifice. May we leave such a legacy for our great-great-grandchildren, for the glory of God.

BIBLIOGRAPHY AND SUGGESTED READING

Amos, Gary T. *Defending the Declaration.* Brentwood, TN: Wolgemuth & Hyatt Publishers, Inc., 1989.

Bahnsen, Greg L. and Kenneth L. Gentry, Jr. *The Break Up of Dispensational Theology.* Tyler, TX: Institute for Christian Economics, 1989.

Burkett, Larry. *The Coming Economic Earthquake.* Chicago, IL: Moody Press, 1991.

Chilton, David. *Paradise Restored: A Biblical Theology of Dominion.* Tyler, TX: Institute for Christian Economics, 1985.

Conway, John S. *The Nazi Persecution of the Churches, 1933-1945.* New York, NY: Basic Books, 1968.

DeMar, Gary. *America's Christian History: The Untold Story.* Atlanta, GA: American Vision Publishers, Inc., 1993.

Dillon, Merton L. *The Abolitionists.* De Kalb, IL: Northern Illinois University Press, 1974.

Figgie, Harry E. *Bankruptcy—1995: The Coming Collapse of America and How to Stop It.* New York, NY: Little, Brown, 1992.

Grant, George. *Grand Illusions: The Legacy of Planned Parenthood.* Brentwood, TN: Wolgemuth & Hyatt, Publishers, Inc., 1988.

Grant, George. *Third Time Around: A History of the Pro-Life Movement from the First Century to the Present.* Brentwood, TN: Wolgemuth & Hyatt, Publishers, Inc., 1991.

Hyde, Douglas. *Dedication and Leadership: Learning From the Communists.* Notre Dame, IN: University of Notre Dame Press, 1966.

Jackley, John L. *Hill Rat: Blowing the Lid Off Congress.* Washington, DC: Regnery Gateway (distributed by Nation   Book Network, Lanham, MD), 1992.

Manchester, William. *The Last Lion, Winston Spencer Churchill: Alone, 1932-1940.* New York, NY: Little, Brown, 1988.

McIlhenny, Chuck and Donna, with Frank York. *When the Wicked Seize a City: A Grim Look at the Future and a Warn ing to the Church.* Lafayette, LA: Huntington House Publishers, 1993.

Morris, Edmund. *The Rise of Theodore Roosevelt.* New York, NY: Coward, McCann & Geoghegan, 1979.

Murray, Iain H. *The Puritan Hope: A Study in Revival and the Interpretation of History.* Carlisle, PA: Banner of Truth, 1971.

Niemöller, Martin. *Of Guilt and Hope.* Translated by Renee Spodheim. New York, NY: Philosophical Library, Inc., n.d.

North, Gary. *Political Polytheism: The Myth of Pluralism.* Tyler, TX: Institute for Christian Economics, 1989.

Stern, Philip M. *The Best Congress Money Can Buy.* New York, NY: Pantheon Books, 1988.

Terry, Randall A. *Operation Rescue.* Springdale, PA: Whitaker House, 1988.

Terry, Randall A. *Accessory To Murder: The Enemies, Allies, And Accomplices To The Death of Our Culture.* Brentwood, TN: Wolgemuth & Hyatt, Publishers, Inc., 1990.

Whitehead, John W. *An American Dream.* Westchester, IL: Crossway Books, 1987.

Wurmbrand, Richard. *Tortured for Christ.* Middlebury, IN: Living Sacrifice Books, 1985.

Notes

Introduction

1. S. Herman, *The Rebirth of the German Church* (London, 1946), 137, quoted in John S. Conway, *The Nazi Persecution of the Churches, 1933-45* (New York: Basic Books, 1968), 332.

Chapter One: In the Slammer

1. Hermann Rauschning, *Hitler Speaks* (London: n.p., 1939), 59, quoted in John S. Conway, *The Nazi Persecution of the Churches, 1933-45* (New York: Basic Books, 1968), 332.

2. Conway, *The Nazi Persecution*, 71.

Chapter Two: Visit from the Theological Twilight Zone

1. H. Buchanheim, *Glaubenskrise im Dritten Reich* (Stuttgart, 1953), 51, quoted in John S. Conway, *The Nazi Persecution of the Churches, 1933-45* (New York: Basic Books, 1968), 11.

2. G. van Norden, *Kriche in der Krise* (Dusseldorf, 1963), 181, quoted in Conway, *The Nazi Persecution*, 11-12.

3. Evangelische Nachrichten (21/2/1934), quoted in Wilhelm Niemöller, *Kampf und Zeugnis* (Bielefeld, 1948), 487, and Conway, *The Nazi Persecution*, 234.

4. G. Lewy, *The Catholic Church and Nazi Germany* (Boston: n.p., 1964), 295, quoted in Conway, *The Nazi Persecution*, 261.

Chapter Three: God's Law Is Supreme

1. Nathanial Micklem, *National Socialism and the Roman Catholic Church* (London, 1939), 163-164, quoted in John S. Conway, *The Nazi Persecution of the Churches, 1933-45* (New York: Basic Books, 1968), 151.

2. Bundesarchiv, Akten Der Reichskanzlei, 43, II, 156, quoted in Conway, *The Nazi Persecution*, 161.

3. Conway, *The Nazi Persecution*, 86.

Chapter Four: 666, Anyone?

1. Dokumente der deutschen Politik, vol. IV, ed. Hohlfeld (Berlin, 1954), 30, quoted in John S. Conway, *The Nazi Persecution of the Churches, 1933-45* (New York: Basic Books, 1968), 20.

2. Nathanial Micklem, *National Socialism and the Roman Catholic Church* (London, 1939), 204, quoted in Conway, *The Nazi Persecution*, 185.

Chapter Five: The Idol of Reputation

1. Hermann Rauschning, *Hitler Speaks* (London, 1939), 61, quoted in John S. Conway, *The Nazi Persecution of the Churches, 1933-45* (New York: Basic Books, 1968), 103.

2. Conway, *The Nazi Persecution,* 134.

Chapter Six: Just Preach the Gospel

1. *Volkischer Beobachter,* (5 August 1935), quoted in John S. Conway, *The Nazi Persecution of the Churches, 1933-45* (New York: Basic Books, 1968), 114-115.

2. Conway, *The Nazi Persecution,* 78.

Chapter Seven: The Battle of Allegiances

1. Speech to a Party rally (11 September 1935), quoted in John S. Conway, *The Nazi Persecution of the Churches, 1933-45* (New York: Basic Books, 1968), 104-105.

2. Conway, *The Nazi Persecution,* 96-97.

3. James D. Richardson, *A Compilation of the Messages and Papers of the Presidents,* I (Bureau of National Literature and Art, 1911), 212.

4. Gary DeMar, *America's Christian History* (Atlanta, GA: American Vision Publishers, Inc., 1993), 58.

5. Ibid., 60.

6. Ibid.

7. Ibid.

8. Noah Brooks, *Men of Achievement: Statesmen* (New York: Charles Scribner's Sons, 1904), 317, quoted in George Grant, *Third Time Around: A History of the Pro-Life Movement from the First Century to the Present* (Brentwood, TN: Wolgemuth & Hyatt Publishers, Inc., 1991), 118.

9. David L. Johnson, *Theodore Roosevelt: American Monarch* (Philadelphia: American History Sources, 1981), 44, quoted in Grant, *Third Time,* 118-119.

10. Richardson, *A Compilation of the Messages,* 258-259.

Chapter Eight: Culturally Illiterate, Socially Irrelevant

1. *The Persecution of the Catholic Church in the Third Reich* (London, 1940), 118, quoted in John S. Conway, *The Nazi Persecution of the Churches, 1933-45* (New York: Basic Books, 1968), 178.

Chapter Nine: The Magic Wand

1. F. Zipfel, *Kirchenkampf in Deutschland* (Berlin, 1965), 450-451, quoted in John S. Conway, *The Nazi Persecution of the Churches, 1933-45* (New York: Basic Books, 1968), 177.

2. Nazi Party Directive No. 79/39 (12 April 1939) from the files of the American Document Centere, Berlin, quoted in Conway, *The Nazi Persecution,* 366.

3. Hermann Rauschning, *Hitler Speaks* (London, 1939), 237, quoted in Conway, *The Nazi Persecution,* 152.

Chapter 10: The War of the Testaments

1. John S. Conway, *The Nazi Persecution of the Churches, 1933-45* (New York: Basic Books, 1968), 52.

2. BA. Schu 245/192 in H. Buchheim, *Glaubenskrise im Dritten Reich* (Stuttgart, 1953), 85, quoted in Conway, *The Nazi Persecution,* 181-182.

Chapter Eleven: Battling in Houston

1. H. Moeller, *Katholische Kirche und Nationalsozialismus* (Munich, 1963), quoted in John S. Conway, *The Nazi Persecution of the Churches, 1933-45* (New York: Basic Books, 1968), 65.

2. Conway, *The Nazi Persecution*, 114.

3. Ibid., 69-70.

Chapter Twelve: Battling with Congress

1. Evangelische Nachrichten (21/2/1934) in W. Niemöller, *Kampf und Zeugnis* (Bielefeld, 1948), 261, quoted in John S. Conway, *The Nazi Persecution of the Churches, 1933-45* (New York: Basic Books, 1968), 113.

2. Ibid., 267.

3 *The Persecution of the Catholic Church in the Third Reich* (London, 1940), 87, quoted in Conway, *The Nazi Persecution*, 123.

Chapter Thirteen: Battling with Clinton

1. S. W. Herman, *It's Your Souls We Want* (London, 1942), 15, quoted in John S. Conway, *The Nazi Persecution of the Churches, 1933-45* (New York: Basic Books, 1968), 202.

2. John S. Conway, *The Nazi Persecution of the Churches, 1933-45* (New York: Basic Books, 1968), 95.

3. G. Lewy, *The Catholic Church and Nazi Germany* (Boston: n.p.,1964), 174-175, quoted in Conway, *The Nazi Persecution*, 157.

Chapter Fourteen: Battling the Internal Revenue Service

1. John S. Conway, *The Nazi Persecution of the Churches, 1933-45* (New York: Basic Books, 1968), 174.

2. M. Domarus, *Hitler Reden und Proklamationen 1932-45.* II (Wurzburg: n.p., 1963), 1058-1061, quoted in Conway, *The Nazi Persecution*, 219.

Chapter Fifteen: What Must We Do to Be Saved?

1. Martin Niemöller, *Of Guilt and Hope* (New York: Philosophical Library, n.d.), 16.

2. Martin Niemöller, Evangelische Nachrichten (21/2/1934), in Wilhelm Niemöller, *Kampf and Zeugnis der Bekennenden Kirche* (Bielefeld, 1948), 282, quoted in Conway, *The Nazi Persecution* (New York: Basic Books, 1968), 136.

3. Theodore Roosevelt, *Foes of Our Own Household* (New York: Charles Scribner's Sons, 1917, 1926), 3, quoted in George Grant, *Third Time Around: A History of the Pro-Life Movement from the First Century to the Present* (Brentwood, TN: Wolgemuth & Hyatt, Publishers, Inc., 1991), 116.

Resistance Press Releases

Accessory to Murder
by Randall Terry

This book is a biting exposé of the forces that the most visible pro-life crusader in America has met face-to-face. And, it was written from the vantage point many activists throughout history have had to face—prison.

Unlike anything you have ever read, this book draws the battle lines between life and death and the forces of righteousness and unrighteousness. It reveals the horror and calculated cruelty of the people and organizations that are promoting moral anarchy in America.

Terry chronicles his findings and personal experiences with Planned Parenthood, the American Civil Liberties Union, and the National Organization for Women. He uncovers the overt bias of every major television network and most major print media in maintaining an ongoing anti-Christian stand.

With undeniable facts, Randall Terry exposes the accessories to the murder of our children, the destruction of our culture and the failure of the Church to take action.

ISBN 0-943497-78-7 $8.00 ea.

Operation Rescue
by Randall Terry

You can help stop the abortion holocaust in America!

"Something is happening in the Pro-Life Movement and I believe it is a direct answer to prayer... I encourage the body of Christ to join in Operation Rescue as salt and light to our communities. We must live our faith, prayerfully and in a Christ-like manner, putting action behind our words."

Dr. D. James Kennedy

"I commend Randy Terry for his boldness and applaud the goal of Operation Rescue to save the lives of one and half million unborn children who are slaughtered in our land every year."

Pat Robertson

"I sanction and endorse operation rescue and its use of non-violent civil disobedience as a means of putting an end to abortion in this country. I strongly urge the reading of this book and prayerful consideration of getting involved in this movement."

Jerry Falwell
ISBN 0-88368-209-5 $8.00 ea.

To order books listed above, send check or money order in the amount of the book order to:

Resistance Press Book Order
P.O. Box 600
Windsor, NY 13865

Prices listed above include postage and handling.

MORE GOOD BOOKS FROM
HUNTINGTON HOUSE PUBLISHERS

RECENT RELEASES

Prescription Death—
Compassionate Killers in the Medical Profession
by Dr. Reed Bell with Frank York

Is your doctor a compassionate killer? Will American physicians become like the Nazi doctors who killed their patients in order to solve political, social, and economic problems? YES—says Dr. Reed Bell, pediatrician and bioethicist. The cultural climate is perfect for these Nazi-like solutions! Dr. Bell details the roots of the pro-death ethic in medicine—from ancient Greece and Nazi Germany to present day practices.

Trade paper ISBN 1-56384-016-2 $9.99

Loyal Opposition:
A Christian Response to the Clinton Agenda
by John Eidsmoe

The night before the November 1992 election, a well-known evangelist claims to have had a dream. In this dream, he says, God told him that Bill Clinton would be elected president, and Christians should support his presidency. What are we to make of this? If someone claims God spoke to him in a dream, do we accept his claim on blind faith? And, what are we to make of Bill Clinton? Does it follow that, because God allowed Clinton to be president; therefore, God wants Clinton to be president? Does God want everything that God allows? Is it possible for an event to occur even though that event displeases God? How do we stand firm in our opposition to the administration's proposals when those proposals contradict biblical values? And, how do we organize and work effectively for constructive action to restore our nation to basic values?

Trade paper ISBN 1-56384-044-8 $7.99

The Extermination of Christianity: A Tyranny of Consensus

by Paul C. Schenck with Robert L. Schenck

Paul Schenck offers convincing evidence that a militant and secular coalition is using every available means to purge Christianity from the American landscape. If you are a Christian, you might be surprised to discover that popular music, television, and motion pictures are consistently depicting you as: a stooge, a hypocrite, a charlatan, a racist, an anti-Semite, mentally ill, or a con artist. If you are a student in a public high school, you might be shocked to learn that you could be prohibited from bringing your Bible to school, expelled for giving Christian literature to a classmate, or arrested and taken to jail for praying on school grounds. The preparation for Christian persecution is not at all unlike the preparation Hitler employed when preparing for the persecution of the Jews. This book is a catalogue of anti-Christian propaganda—a record of persecution before it happens.

Trade Quality ISBN 1-56384-050-0 $9.99

A Jewish Conservative Looks at Pagan America

by Don Feder

With eloquence and insight that rival contemporary commentators and essayists of antiquity, Don Feder's pen finds his targets in the enemies of God, family, and American tradition and morality. Deftly . . . delightfully . . . the master allegorist and Titan with a typewriter brings clarity to the most complex sociological issues and invokes giggles and wry smiles from both followers and foes. Feder is Jewish to the core, and he finds in his Judaism no inconsistency with an American Judeo-Christian ethic. Questions of morality plague school administrators, district court judges, senators, congressmen, parents, and employers; they are wrestling for answers in a "changing world." But Feder challenges the evolving society theory and directs inquirers to the original books of wisdom: the Torah and the Bible.

ISBN Quality Trade Paper 1-56384-036-7 $9.99
ISBN Hardcover 1-56384-037-5 $19.99

Political Correctness: The Cloning of the American Mind

by David Thibodaux, Ph.D.

The author, professor of literature at the University of Southwestern Louisiana, confronts head-on the movement that is now being called Political Correctness. Political Correctness, says Thibodaux, "is an umbrella under which advocates of civil rights, gay and lesbian rights, feminism, and environmental causes have gathered." To incur the wrath of these groups, one only has to disagree with them on political, moral, or social issues. To express traditionally Western concepts in universities today can result in not only ostracism, but even suspension. (According to a recent "McNeil-Lehrer News Hour" report, one student was suspended for discussing the reality of the moral law with an avowed homosexual. He was reinstated only after he apologized.)

ISBN Quality Trade Paper 1-56384-026-X $9.99
ISBN Hardcover 1-56384-033-2 $18.99

When the Wicked Seize a City
by Chuck & Donna McIlhenny with Frank York

A highly publicized lawsuit . . . a house fire-bombed in the night . . . the shatter of windows smashed by politically (and wickedly) motivated vandals cuts into the night . . . All because Chuck McIlhenny voiced God's condemnation of a behavior and life-style and protested the destruction of society that results from its practice. That behavior is homosexuality, and that life-style is the gay culture. This book explores: the rise of gay power and what it will mean if Christians do not organize and prepare for the battle; homosexual attempts to have the American Psychiatric Association remove pedophilia from the list of mental illnesses—now they want homophobia declared a disorder.

ISBN 1-56384-024-3 $9.99

Dinosaurs and the Bible
by David W. Unfred

Every reader, young and old, will be fascinated by this ever-mysterious topic—exactly what happened to the dinosaurs? Author David Unfred draws a very descriptive picture of the history and fate of the dinosaurs, using the Bible as a reference guide. Did dinosaurs really exist? Does the Bible mention dinosaurs? What happened to dinosaurs, or are there some still living awaiting discovery?

ISBN Hardcover 0-910311-70-6 $12.99

America Betrayed
by Marlin Maddoux

This hard-hitting book exposes the forces in our country which seek to destroy the family, the schools, our culture, and our values. The author details exactly how the news media manipulates your mind. Maddoux is the host of the popular national radio talk show, "Point of View."

ISBN 0-910311-18-8 $6.99

Kinsey, Sex and Fraud: The Indoctrination of a People
by Dr. Judith A. Reisman and Edward Eichel

Kinsey, Sex and Fraud describes the research of Alfred Kinsey which shaped Western society's beliefs and understanding of the nature of human sexuality. His unchallenged conclusions are taught at every level of education—elementary, high school and college—and quoted in textbooks as undisputed truth.

The authors clearly demonstrate that Kinsey's research involved illegal experimentations on several hundred children. The survey was carried out on a non-representative group of Americans, including disproportionately large numbers of sex offenders, prostitutes, prison inmates and exhibitionists.

ISBN Hardcover 0-910311-20-X $19.99

"Soft Porn" Plays Hardball
by Dr. Judith A. Reisman

With amazing clarity, the author demonstrates that pornography imposes on society a view of women and children that encourages violence and sexual abuse. As crimes against women and children increase to alarming proportions, it's of paramount importance that we recognize the cause of this violence. Pornography should be held accountable for the havoc it has wreaked in our homes and our country.

ISBN Trade Paper 0-910311-65-X $8.99
ISBN Hardcover 0-910311-92-7 $16.95

Don't Touch That Dial:
The Impact of the Media on Children and the Family
by Barbara Hattemer & Robert Showers

Men and women without any stake in the outcome of the war between the pornographers and our families have come to the qualified, professional agreement that media does have an effect on our children—an effect that is devastatingly significant. Highly respected researchers, psychologists, and sociologists join the realm of pediatricians, district attorneys, parents, teachers, pastors, and community leaders—who have diligently remained true to the fight against filthy media—in their latest comprehensive critique of the modern media establishment (i.e., film, television, print, art, curriculum).

ISBN Quality Trade Paper 1-56384-032-4 $9.99
ISBN Hardcover 1-56384-035-9 $19.99

Heresy Hunters
by James Spencer

An alarming error is sweeping the Christian Church. A small, self-appointed band is confusing Bible-scholarship with character assassination. These heresy hunters fail to distinguish between genuine error and Christian diversity and turn on their brothers in an ungodly feeding frenzy. Using secular slash-and-burn journalism, the heresy hunters resort to personal assault and innuendo to remove those with whom they disagree from the ministry.

Trade Paper ISBN 1-56384-042-1 $8.99

America: Awaiting the Verdict
by Mike Fuselier

We are a nation stricken with an infectious disease. The disease is called betrayal—we are a nation that has denied, rejected, and betrayed our Christian past. The symptoms of the disease are many and multiplying daily. Mike Fuselier thus encourages Americans to return to the faith of their founding fathers—the faith upon which our law and government rests—or suffer the consequences. To prove that our forebearers were in no way attempting to establish a secular state, as contended by secular humanists, the author presents oft-forgotten but crucial evidence to fortify his—and all Christians'—case.

ISBN 1-56384-034-0 $5.99

Trojan Horse-
How the New Age Movement Infiltrates the Church
by Samantha Smith and Brenda Scott

The authors attempt to demonstrate that Madeleine L'Engle (well-known author and speaker) has been and continues to be a major New Age source of entry into the church. Because of her radical departure from traditional Christian theology, Madeleine L'Engle's writings have sparked a wave of controversy across the nation. She has been published and promoted by numerous magazines including *Today's Christian Woman, Christianity Today,* and many others.

Trade Paper ISBN 1-56384-040-5 $9.99

Christ Returns to the Soviets:
A Revolution of the Heart
by Greg Gulley and Kim Parker

A rebirth of Christianity is occurring at this very moment. It is occurring on a large segment of our planet—the former Soviet Union. For 70 years, the possession of a Bible would bring a prison sentence and the loss of family and job. But, now these people are hungry for the Truth. Years of communism and atheism have caused their souls to ache. Since 1990, the members of New Life Ministries have witnessed first hand this century's most historic events as the walls have come tumbling down in the former Soviet Union. New Life teams have been given unprecedented freedom to evangelize. They have appeared on Soviet television, in theaters, public schools, and Pioneer Youth Camps. (These camps were used for Communist indoctrination.) The events in this book are true and are evidence of God's hand moving across history.

Trade Paper ISBN 1-56384-041-3 $9.99

The Subtle Serpent:
New Age in the Classroom
by Darylann Whitemarsh & Bill Reisman

There is a new morality being taught to our children in public schools. Without the consent or even awareness of parents, educators and social engineers are aggressively introducing new moral codes to our children. In most instances, these new moral codes contradict the traditional values. Darylann Whitemarsh (a 1989 Teacher of the Year) and Bill Reisman (educator and expert on the occult) combine their knowledge to expose the deliberate madness occurring in our public schools.

ISBN 1-56384-016-2 $9.99

False Security:
Has the New Age Given Us a False Hope?
by Jerry Parks

The Great Tribulation! Wars, famine, pestilence, persecution—these are just some of the frightful events in the future of the world. Are they in your future? For centuries, the prophets searched the Scriptures for the timing of the first coming of the Messiah; now we watch and wait for the Second Coming of Christ and everything that foreshadows it. In *False Security: Has the New Age Given Us a False Hope?* author Jerry Parks discusses a relatively recent teaching that has infiltrated the Church, giving many a false hope. When will the Rapture occur? Be prepared to examine your own beliefs and clear up many of the questions you may have about the close of this age.

ISBN 1-56384-012-X $9.99

Exposing the AIDS Scandal
by Dr. Paul Cameron

Where do you turn when those who control the flow of information in this country withhold the truth? Why is the national media hiding facts from the public? Can AIDS be spread in ways we're not being told? Finally, a book that gives you a total account for the AIDS epidemic, and what steps can be taken to protect yourself. What you don't know can kill you!

ISBN 0-910311-52-8 $7.99

Blessings of Liberty:
Restoring the City on the Hill
by Charles Heath

The author believes Liberalism is destroying our nation. If we continue to do nothing, say Heath, the traditional family values that we cherish and the kind of government envisioned by our founding fathers will cease to exist. Heath presents a coherent case for limited government, decentralized and self-governing communities, and a return to traditional values. Conservatism, he continues, has its premise in the book of Genesis. It is the only viable philosophy capable of addressing and solving today's problems.

Trade Paper ISBN 1-56384-005-7 $8.99

Deadly Deception
by Jim Shaw & Tom McKenney

For the first time the 33 degree ritual is made public! Learn of the "secrets" and "deceptions" that are practiced daily around the world. Find out why Freemasonry teaches that it is the true religion, that all other religions are but corrupted and perverted forms of Freemasonry. If you know anyone in the Masonic movement, you must read this book.

ISBN 0-910311-54-4 $7.99

The Devil's Web
by Pat Pulling with Kathy Cawthon

This explosive exposé presents the first comprehensive guide to childhood and adolescent occult involvement. Written by a nationally recognized occult crime expert, the author explains how the violent occult underworld operates and how they stalk and recruit our children, teen-agers, and young adults for their evil purposes.

ISBN Trade Paper 0-910311-59-5 $8.99
ISBN Hardcover 0-910311-63-3 $16.99

THE SALT SERIES

Exposing the AIDS Scandal
by Paul Cameron, M.D.
AIDS is 100 percent fatal all of the time. There are believed to be over 1,500,000 people in the United States carrying the AIDS virus. The ever-growing number of cases compels us to question whether there will be a civilization in twenty years.

ISBN 1-56384-023-5 $2.99

Inside the New Age Nightmare
by Randall Baer
Are your children safe from the New Age movement? This former New Age leader, one of the world's foremost experts in crystals, brings to light the darkest of the darkness that surrounds the New Age movement. The week that Randall Baer's original book was released, he met with a puzzling and untimely death—his car ran off a mountain pass. His death is still regarded as suspicious.

ISBN 1-56384-022-7 $2.99

The Question of Freemasonry
by Ed Decker
Blood oaths, blasphemy, and illegal activity—in this day and age it's hard to believe these aberrations still exist; this booklet demonstrates that the Freemasons are not simply a "goodwill," community-oriented organization.

ISBN 1-56384-020-0 $2.99

To Moroni With Love
by Ed Decker
Readers are led through the deepest of the Mormon church doctrines and encouraged to honestly determine whether the words can be construed as heresy in light of the true, unadulterated language of the Bible. Decker reveals shocking material that has caused countless Mormons to question the church leaders and abandon Mormonism's false teachings.

ISBN 1-56384-021-9 $2.99

ORDER THESE HUNTINGTON HOUSE BOOKS !

* _New Title_

Shipping and Handling _____

Total _____

AVAILABLE AT BOOKSTORES EVERYWHERE or order direct from:
Huntington House Publishers • P.O. Box 53788 • Lafayette, LA 70505
Send check/money order. For faster service use VISA/MASTERCARD
call toll-free 1-800-749-4009.

Add: Freight and handling, $3.50 for the first book ordered, and $.50 for each additional
book up to 5 books.

Enclosed is $_____ including postage.

VISA/MASTERCARD#_____ Exp. Date_____

Name_____ Phone: (   )_____

Address_____

City, State, Zip_____